The Leopard Gecko,
Eublepharis macularius, in Captivity
by Robbie Hamper

Professional Breeders Series

E C O

© 2004 by ECO Herpetological Publishing & Distribution.

ISBN 0-9713197-8-2

Copies available from:

ECO Herpetological Publishing & Distribution
915 Seymour
Lansing, MI 48906 USA
telephone: 517.487.5595
fax: 517.371.2709
email: ecoorders@hotmail.com
website: http://www.reptileshirts.com

Zoo Book Sales
P. O. Box 305
Lanesboro, MN 55900
507.467.8733
http://www.zoobooksales.com

Elegant Reptile Images
http://www.pythons.com/hamper
fax: 614.459.4261

LIVING ART publishing
http://www.livingartpublishing.com

Design and layout by Russ Gurley.
Cover design by Rafael Porrata.
Printed in China

Front Cover: The incredible new Sun Glow Leopard Gecko. Photo by Craig Stewart of The Urban Gecko.
Back Cover: A stunning Hypo Snow Leopard Gecko. Photo by Craig Stewart of The Urban Gecko.

ACKNOWLEDGEMENTS

Dedicated to – My Parents, Emerson and Louise Helman - whose inspiration, encouragement, and love allowed me to seek new challenges, to do my best, and to learn something new everyday!

In 1991, looking for my own special reptile project to do, Don, my husband, suggested that I consider Leopard Geckos. I really didn't know what they were as I had never seen one. Leopard Geckos were in the infancy stage of being successfully captive bred and offered for sale. My first colony of Leopard Geckos consisted of 500 tiny hatchlings from Ron and Marilyn Tremper. I immediately became fascinated with them. They always had smiles on their faces, had beautiful yellow and black banding, and were "cute as buttons" with their charming antics.

After 13 years, I still find them interesting, fascinating, and fun. I have been involved with every aspect of raising, caring, breeding, and selling Leopard Geckos. As with any adventure, there are trials, errors, problems to be solved, and long hours of work. However, this is how we learn and the satisfaction gained when we succeed is a thrill. After hatching thousands of Leopard Geckos, each one that emerges is still special and just as exciting as the very first one.

I want to thank Bob and Sheri Ashley of ECO Publishing for asking me to write my second book. I value our friendship and am honored that Bob believes in me and my experience in the field of herpetoculture, especially Leopard Geckos.

A special thank-you goes to Russ Gurley for his work as editor and layout designer. Without his time and effort, this book would not have materialized. Also, to Eric Thiss, of Serpents Tale and Zoo Book Sales, for the book distribution. I am grateful and obliged to my professional Leopard Gecko and African Fat-tail friends who immediately agreed to help by allowing me to photograph their geckos or providing outstanding photographs of their own. The following persons helped to make this book special with their assistance: John and Amy Mack of Reptiles by Mack, always accommodating my requests for photographs and information, my special assistant, John

Mack IV (L. J.) for his help, Bill and Marcia Brant of Gourmet Rodent, Inc., for their knowledge and willingness to help, Albey Scholl of Albey's "Too Cool" Reptiles, Raymond Ditmars Bruckman of Bruckman Geckos, Mark and Kim Bell of Reptile Industries, Alberto Cadolini of A & M Gecko, Lois Durflinger of L & J Reptiles, Ray Hines of Ray Hines Geckos, UK, Bill Love of Blue Chameleon Ventures, Ruben and Glenda Lugo of Taino Reptiles, Jeff Galewood and Jeff Galewood, Jr. of JMG Reptiles, Craig Stewart of The Urban Gecko, Ron and Marilyn Tremper, Andreas Nöllert, Mike Shipp, and Al and Billie Zulich of Harford Reptile Breeding Center.

Most importantly, I would like to express my gratitude to Don, my husband, whose professional expertise and knowledge in all aspects of herpetology has been invaluable. A thank you of love goes to my children and best friends, Shay and Anietra, to my best "buddy" and grandson, Zach, and my sisters, Nancy and Susan. They have always been willing to help and assist with me in any way, especially with compliments and words of encouragement. A very special hug and thank-you to Zach and Taylor, my two wonderful young helpers who feed, water, and give lots of love to the Leopard Geckos. Also, to my in-laws, Bernie, Leona, and Sandy Hamper, whose acceptance and support of me throughout the years is true family devotion.

This is only the beginning of a new era for Leopard Geckos. It is my hope that this Leopard Gecko book will guide and inspire keepers by giving them reliable, useful information on all aspects of keeping and breeding healthy Leopard Geckos and African Fat-tail Geckos.

I am awed at the beautiful new color morphs and mutations presently being produced and feel fortunate to have been a player in the Leopard Gecko "revolution". I hope you will be inspired to stretch your visions and imagination.

In a poem by Robert Frost, called *The Road Not Taken*, he says:

..."two roads diverged in a wood, and I --,
I took the one less traveled by,
And that has made all the difference."

Take the challenge of a less traveled road and make a difference!

Contents

INTRODUCTION

GENERAL INFORMATION

Eublepharis macularius, commonly known as the Leopard Gecko, is probably the most notable gecko in today's pet industry. For years, the Leopard Gecko was imported as just another gecko. It was not until the last decade that Leopard Geckos gained a place of prominence, as not only an ideal pet, but also an ideal breeding project.

Geckos are some of the oldest reptiles to inhabit the Earth. Ancestors of today's Leopard Geckos date back 20 million years. Through evolution and ongoing specialized adaptation, thousands of different gecko species have emerged, each with unique characteristics to ensure survival in their specific habitat. Leopard Geckos have developed physical traits to survive the hot, arid daytime conditions of their natural habitat.

Leopard Geckos are able to get needed moisture from the food they eat, have the ability to efficiently conserve fat and water in their tails, developed a scaly, non-porous skin, and have a dry excretion for minimal water loss. Leopard Geckos, being nocturnal, also conserve water by coming out in the cool nighttime, to eat and to lick any moisture that may accumulate on the surface of rocks or leaves.

All animals are part of a scientific classification system. The classification system, or taxology, describes and defines each animal's characteristics in an orderly format. It is then possible to determine how closely certain groups are related by their similar traits.

Leopard Geckos are classified as the following:

Kingdom – *Animalia*, Phylum – *Chordata*, Class – *Reptilia*, Order – *Squamata,* Suborder – *Sauria*, Immediate Order – *Gekkota*, Family – *Geckkonidae*, Subfamily – *Eublepharine*, Genus - *Eublepharis*, Species – *macularius.*

The Leopard Geckos' subfamily, *Eublepharine*, includes geckos with "moveable eyelids". Geckos in this subfamily also lack toe pads of lamellae. The etymology of the Leopard Geckos scientific name, *Eublepharis macularius,* can be broken down to describe the geckos physical traits as: *Eu* – true, good, *bllephar* – eyelid, *macularis* – spotted.

For the purpose of this book, the common name of Leopard Gecko will be used along with the scientific name, *Eublepharis macularius.* It is important to be familiar with both the scientific and common name of these geckos as they are often used interchangeably.

The goal of this book is to give you useful information on all aspects of Leopard Gecko husbandry. Each chapter will cover specific subjects giving you suggestions and insight on how to best enhance the quality of life of your Leopard Gecko.

Remember: Be a responsible caregiver to your Leopard Gecko and the gecko, in turn, will thank you by giving you many years of pleasure and companionship.

Chapter ONE: THE LEOPARD GECKO IN NATURE

Eublepharis macularius, or the Leopard Gecko as it is commonly known, has become the ideal gecko for a pet or for a breeding program. For many years, Leopard Geckos were wild-caught and exported from Afghanistan and Pakistan. However, Leopard Geckos, as we know them today, look quite different from the original imports due to selective breeding and the quality of care and maintenance the species has received, producing healthy and often colorful animals.

Dry, rocky habitat of the Leopard Gecko. Photo by Andreas Nolleit.

The first mention of a Leopard Gecko found and documented in nature was in 1903, by N.A. Zarudny, a Russian ornithologist. While traveling in Persia, now Iran, Zarudny collected two lizard specimens and identified them as members of the genus *Eublepharis* and the species, *macularius*. However, the specimens he collected were lost before a physical and scientific identification could be made at the science center in St. Peterburg, Russia. Subsequently, *Eublepharis* populations have been located in the same general area but have been identified as different species, not *macularius*.

Typical Eublepharis habitat in the Middle East. Photo by Phillip Groll, SMSgt.

Eublepharis macularius, the Leopard Gecko, as we know them today in the pet industry, are some of the most popular geckos kept as pets. However, Leopard Geckos found in the wild are often drab and dull and have a darker background coloration with more spotting and are typically not as calm. Today's captive-bred Leopard Geckos are found in a myriad of patterns and colors. Many unique morphs have been created by selective breeding and unexpected mutations.

In nature, the Leopard Gecko is found in Afghanistan, Pakistan, parts of Iran, and India. They are found in hot, rocky, and semiarid desert areas with a terrain of sandy gravel, hard clay soil, and sparse vegetation of grasses and shrubs. In many of these regions, the summer temperatures get quite high, ranging from 104° F (40° C) during the day to a low of 77° F (25° C) at night. Winter in these regions is usually from December to late February with temperatures ranging from 59° F (15° C) during the day to a low of 41° F (5° C) at night. Leopard Geckos remain under-ground during this time in semi-hibernation, relying on the stored fat reserve in their tails for nourishment. This cooling period also prepares them for their breeding season once they emerge from dormancy.

"Normal" Leopard Geckos are quite social animals, often living in colonies in nature. Photo by Robbie Hamper.

Leopard Geckos are social animals that often live in large colonies in nature. They are nocturnal, sleeping during the day and becoming active at night. As carnivores, Leopard Geckos search for food such as insects, worms, or spiders. Leopard Gecko predators include snakes, birds, or foxes. The swiftness of Leopard Geckos, in addition to their keen sense of sight and hearing at night, help them to escape from their enemies. During the daytime, Leopard Geckos stay secluded underground in dark burrows or holes. The elongated body and short limbs of leopard geckos allow them to easily slip between cracks and into crevices for safety. With drab coloration and knobby skin, leopard geckos are masters at camouflaging themselves whenever they are out roaming around.

Leopard Geckos rely on their ability to store excess fat in their tails when their food supply is abundant and easily obtained. However, living in a hot desert area where periods of droughts can occur, Leopard Geckos must rely on this stored reserve to survive. They also eat their own shed skin which gives them added protein

A beautiful Super-Hypo Tangerine (Baldy) Leopard Gecko courtesy of Taino Reptiles. Photo by Robbie Hamper.

and nutrition. Leopard Geckos require an adequate amount of calcium in captivity, but it is not known what they eat in nature that supplies this calcium. Since they are found in a desert habitat with sandy gravel, perhaps something in the sand provides this needed calcium. Research projects are needed for long-term studies of Leopard Geckos in their natural habitats, but due to environmental destruction and civil unrest in these areas, studies are limited or non-existent.

Leopard Geckos, being hardy creatures, have adapted to the harsh environmental conditions of their habitat by utilizing optimum resources to assure the continued longevity of their species in the wild.

Chapter TWO: ANATOMY

Leopard Geckos, such as this albinistic individual, have large beautiful, multi-variegated eyes. Photo by Don Hamper.

There are over 800 species of geckos on Earth. Each one is unique and displays its own distinguishing features and characteristics in size, color, personality, diet, and habitat. Some gecko species have retractable eyelids and small claws for climbing and digging, while others have fixed eyelids and adhesive lamellae-covered pads that allow them to climb and to cling to any surface. Gecko species are also identified as being either diurnal (coming out in the daytime and sleeping at night) or nocturnal (coming out only during the evening and nighttime and sleeping during the daytime).

Leopard Geckos belong to the group of geckos that are nocturnal and have eyelids. They get their common name from the dark spotted leopard-like pigmentation occurring in their skin. Leopard Geckos, originally imported from the wild, have become one of the most successfully bred lizards in captivity. Through selective breeding and genetic mutations, many new and beautiful pattern and color morphs have been developed.

An unusual Mack Paradox Leopard Gecko hatchling. Photo by Robbie Hamper. Animal courtesy of Reptiles by Mack.

Body

Overall body length of hatchling Leopard Geckos are approximately 2 ½" to 3 ½" (6.5 cm to 8.4 cm) weighing an average of 3 grams. As adults, Leopard Geckos attain a length of 8" to 11" (20.5 cm to 27.5 cm) and weigh an average of 45 to 65 grams. The body is elongated and flexible, making it easy for them to move in and out of small spaces. A small, triangle-shaped head is attached to the gecko's body by a very short neck.

Leopard Geckos have four thin, short legs with five toes on each foot, enabling them to be quick and agile. At the end of each spider-like toe, a small nail is attached which makes it possible for the Leopard Gecko to easily climb twigs or rocks. Without the adhesive lamellae pads, they are not able climb up vertical surfaces.

One of the most notable aspects of the Leopard Gecko is its tail. Healthy Leopard Geckos have a thick, fat tail that is approximately the same length as the body and the width of the neck. If a

Leopard Gecko loses its tail, it is able to regenerate a new tail, but the re-grown tail never has the same appearance as the original tail.

Skin

A Super Hypo Tangerine (Baldy) shows the typical small bumps which give Leopard Geckos a rough, textured look. Photo by Albey Scholl of Albey's "Too Cool" Reptiles.

Leopard Geckos have a skin covered with small bumps, giving them a slightly rough look in appearance and texture. The skin on the ventral surface of the Leopard Gecko's body is very thin and transparent making it very smooth to touch. The skin is also very durable, giving Leopard Geckos ample protection in the wild from the rough sand and rock terrain.

Since these geckos have a tougher skin that is not extremely fragile, they can be more easily handled without causing tearing or injury to the gecko.

The skin of Leopard Geckos, similar to other geckos, consists of two layers, the dermis and epidermis. As the Leopard Gecko grows, it will periodically shed the "old" outgrown skin to reveal a new brighter colored one. Just before shedding, the gecko's skin appears dull with a grayish color as it starts to loosen. When the old skin becomes completely separated from the new, the gecko will use its mouth to pull it off in patches. Leopard Geckos will proceed to eat and to swallow the skin completely.

The process of swallowing a shed skin is called "ceratophagia" which means "horn-eating". Ceratophagia is possibly a defense mechanism for geckos. By eating the shed skin, no scent markers are left behind for potential predators to discover. Ingesting the skin possibly allows the Leopard Gecko to utilize beneficial nutrients needed for their growth and health.

Eyes

Leopard Geckos, like other species of geckos, have large beautiful, multi-variegated eyes that are stationary and located on the

A "tasty little meal". A Leopard Gecko shedding its skin and eating it. Photo by Robbie Hamper.

side of the head. Leopard Geckos have a well-developed sense of sight. Being nocturnal, they have pupils that open up quite wide at nighttime, maximizing their ability to see while searching for their food and functioning in the dark. During the daytime or in light, the pupils become vertical slits with a few small pinholes to allow only a minimal amount of light to enter into the eyes.

The irises of Leopard Geckos are a beautiful variegated golden-brown color. Like other *Eublepharis* species, they have moveable eyelids that enable them to close their eyes while sleeping. For more protection, the eye is covered with a thin membrane of skin that will shed during the shedding process. Leopard Geckos, at times, will also lick their eyes to keep them moistened or cleaned.

The Leopard Gecko

Ears

Leopard Geckos have extremely well-developed ears which give them a keen sense of hearing. With no external projections, the Leopard Geckos' ears are openings on either side of the head. A tympanic membrane, resembling an eardrum, covers the openings to protect the ear. Leopard Geckos appear to first locate their live prey, such as crickets, mealworms, or waxworms, with their ears, then key-in with their eyes to make an accurate catch. With a keen sense of hearing and eyesight, Leopard Geckos have an added advantage to alert them to danger during dark nights while roaming around and searching for food.

Smell and Taste

Leopard Geckos appear to also have a well-developed sense of smell and taste. In the wild, living in rough rocky terrain, these well-developed senses are essential to a gecko's search for food and survival. Hatchling geckos readily eat small mealworms and crickets indicating their sense of smell and taste is already well developed. Crickets, mealworms and waxworms probably mirror closely the diet Leopard Geckos eat in the wild.

Voice

Leopard Geckos are capable of making sounds but generally don't vocalize. However, hatchlings and adults will make a hissing sound when they feel threatened, startled, or scared. It is probably a defense mechanism to warn or scare off possible predators.

Tail

Leopard Geckos have one of the most unique and fascinating tails of all the gecko species. Healthy Leopard Geckos have thick, fleshy tails that are made up of muscle, bone, fat and water. The Leopard Gecko is able to store reserve fat in the tail. In the wild, they probably experience a shortage of food during certain times of the year. Through adaptation, the Leopard Geckos' tail has developed the ability to store precious food reserves. In captivity, a Leopard Gecko with a thin tail is an indication that the gecko is

Leopard Geckos with regenerated tails. Photo by Robbie Hamper.

not receiving proper nutrition and care and is not healthy.

Leopard Geckos have the ability to autotomize, or purpose-fully detach their tails. This is a natural defense mechanism and causes no harm to the gecko. Tail detachment can occur if the gecko is attacked by a predator, grabbed by the tail, is bitten during breeding, or is nipped by another gecko during feeding. The detached tail will twitch and wiggle, causing a distraction to a predator while the gecko escapes. Fracture areas in the tailbone enables the gecko to break the bone with muscles, causing the tail to easily separate from the body. Blood loss is minimal as vaso-constriction rapidly occurs.

A Leopard Gecko will immediately start to regenerate its tail, especially since it has just lost a huge amount of stored fat which may be critical to its survival. The regenerated tail never looks the same as the original tail. The new tail will be shorter, bulbous in shape and smoother in texture. If threatening conditions occur again, the regenerated tail will also autotomize.

Thermoregulation

Leopard Geckos are ectothermic which means they must rely entirely on their environment to control the warming or cooling of their bodies. Thermoregulation means that the gecko determines where the temperature is best suited to its needs at any particular time. Leopard Geckos absorb warmth and stock up energy during the daytime while they are sleeping so they can hunt and digest their food during the night. Leopard Geckos, like other animals that thermoregulate, use their food for growth and not for body warmth.

Chapter THREE: CHOOSING YOUR LEOPARD GECKO

Many consider Leopard Geckos to be the perfect reptile pet currently available in the pet trade. They are one of the most abundant captive-produced geckos, with breeders producing thousands each year. Due to genetic selection of colors, patterns, and genetic mutations, new morphs have appeared and are spontaneously appearing. Leopard Geckos are now available in a wide range of beautiful designer

Leopard Geckos make wonderful pets when their simple needs are met properly. Photo by Mike Shipp.

colors, patterns, and even sizes. Leopard Geckos are an ideal pet as they require small cage space, a simple diet, are low maintenance, and extremely docile.

If you are considering a Leopard Gecko as a pet or for a breeding project, there are several important things you should consider before purchasing one. First, you should do research and become as knowledgeable as possible about the behaviors of Leopard Geckos, the proper care and maintenance, and the expected price you will pay for the type of Leopard Gecko you want. It is also a good idea to talk with Leopard Gecko breeders and owners to get their views and opinions about them as a pet. The more informed you are, the easier it will be to decide if a Leopard Gecko is a good pet for you.

Ask yourself if you are choosing a Leopard Gecko because they are cute with a smile on their face, their color and unique designs, or a novelty to impress your friends. These are not the criteria that should be used to make a logical decision about owning a Leopard Gecko. Your decision should be based on how dedicated and responsible you will be in caring for your new pet.

You should also consider the purchase price. Is it in your budget? Can you provide adequate food on a regular basis? Do you have a proper enclosure for housing? Does a Leopard Gecko meet the requirements for a suitable pet and your personality and lifestyle? Even though Leopard Geckos are a relatively low maintenance animal, you must be committed to the animal's everyday care, maintenance, and attention.

Choosing A Leopard Gecko

There are a few basic questions to ask when considering the purchase of a hatchling, sub-adult, or adult Leopard Gecko. The first and most important thing to be concerned with is how the tail looks. It is essential that the tail is plump and fat. This means the gecko is healthy and eating! If the tail is thin and skinny, do not buy the Leopard Gecko. This means the gecko is NOT eating and is not healthy!

1. Does the gecko look, feel, and act healthy?
2. Is the skeletal structure correct without abnormalities due to a calcium deficiency or genetic problem?
3. Is the mouth and jaw shaped correctly, solid, free from injuries, and not soft and spongy?
4. Are the eyes clear and bright with no signs of an infection or abnormality?
5. Is the skin clear of any old skin that did not shed properly, especially on the toes?
6. Are all of the digits and toes normal, none missing or deformed,

and all flexible?

7. Is the tail original or is it regenerated? A regenerated tail is occasionally seen and does not indicate an unhealthy gecko.
8. Is the vent or cloacal opening clear and functioning?
9. Is the gecko docile when held and not trying to bite?
10. Does the gecko seem to take to handling well?

Caution: If you are thinking about buying a hatchling:

Hatchling geckos, just out of their eggs, are about 3" long, approximately one to five days old, and usually have not started to eat. Hatchlings are not an ideal size for beginners who have never raised a Leopard Gecko or other lizards, and are not a good choice for a young child. Hatchlings are little, cute, and relatively inexpensive, however, they are very fragile. Hatchlings need special attention and care to get them to start eating. They cannot be handled or played with – they are quick, can easily lose their tails, and can become stressed! Once stressed, hatchlings usually will not start to eat or will stop if already eating.

Hatchlings should be kept in their own individual containers. If purchasing a hatchling that is displayed in a group situation, be aware that the crowded conditions and bright lights can cause the gecko to already be stressed before you take it home.

The price might be right, but the gecko is probably not starting out in the best manner.

Finding A Gecko

Once you have decided to invest time and money into a Leopard Gecko, it is important to find a source for a healthy animal. There are several options to choose from when searching for a Leopard Gecko.

LEOPARD GECKO BREEDERS

Leopard Geckos have successfully been bred since the 1970s. In 1991, an aberrant gecko randomly hatched which was the beginning of many of the beautiful "designer" geckos presently available. (deVosjoli, Tremper, Viets, and Klingenberg, DVM, 1998).

Presently, many private breeders are successfully producing healthy Leopard Geckos in a great variety of colors, patterns, sizes, and unusual genetic morphs. Where do you start to get a healthy Leopard Gecko? Many private breeders sell their own animals and are well known in the area of herpetoculture. Some private breeders have facilities you can visit and purchase your Leopard Gecko. If you visit a breeder's facility, look at the cleanliness of the facility itself and the cleanliness of the geckos' enclosures. Cleanliness is an important factor in the purchase of a healthy animal. Ask to see a variety of Leopard Geckos in different sizes, colors, sizes, and prices for comparison. This will help you make the best decision on a gecko appropriate for your requirements.

Do not hesitate to ask questions. Questions are important! This is a way to gain valuable knowledge and information about your Leopard Gecko. Credible breeders will take time to answer your questions. They should explain to you how to set up the Leopard Gecko in its new environment, tell you exactly how, when and what to feed your gecko, and the overall general maintenance for a healthy gecko. Be sure to ask if there is a guarantee, and, if there is one, ask what are the specific terms. In case a problem occurs with the Leopard Gecko, you should know if there is a return clause, a replacement only, credit towards another gecko, or a time limit for resolving the problem. If there is a guarantee, is it in writing? If not, request a receipt with the date of purchase for reference.

Leopard Gecko breeders can be located through ads in reptile magazines, through herpetological societies, the Internet, pet shops, or at reptile shows.

REPTILE SHOWS AND EXPOS

One of the best places to purchase a Leopard Gecko is at one of the many professional reptile shows and expos held throughout the United States. At reptile shows and expos, breed-

---

ers and dealers are usually well-known and knowledgeable in the area of reptiles and herpetoculture. Many of the dealers are the breeders of the Leopard Geckos they are offering for sale. You will get to meet and speak with the breeders and look at the many Leopard Geckos they offer for sale and prices. Visiting reptile shows or expos also gives you the opportunity

Both hatchling and adult Leopard Geckos are commonly available at reptile shows. Photo by Robbie Hamper.

to compare the various Leopard Gecko colors, designs, sizes, and prices with other breeders and dealers at the shows. You are able to hand-pick your own very special gecko whether it is for a pet or a breeding project. Selecting your own Leopard Gecko is an advantage over someone else picking one out for you. You will also save the expense of shipping.

The top United States shows are the National Reptile Breeders Expo in Florida, the N.A.R.B.C. shows in Chicago, Philadelphia, and Anaheim, and the E.T.H.S. Conference and Expo in Houston. One of the quality regional shows is the All Ohio Reptile Show held monthly in Columbus, Ohio. There are many other local and regional shows that can be located by checking out the listings in reptile magazines, local herpetological societies, newspapers, and on the Internet.

PET AND SPECIALTY SHOPS

Many pet and specialty shops are now offering Leopard Geckos for sale. These facilities will have only captive bred Leopard Geckos, not wild caught ones. Check for the cleanliness of the shop and the Leopard Geckos' enclosures. Most facilities maintain a clean and healthy environment for their Leopard Geckos, giving them adequate care and a healthy diet. Quality pet and specialty shops are interested in the welfare of the animals they are offering for sale. It is important for these retail facilities to maintain quality animals and to educate the first time buyer of reptiles.

If you purchase a Leopard Gecko at a pet or specialty shop, qualified personnel should be able to adequately answer all of your questions, give you information as to the care and maintenance of the gecko, have available care sheets, books, and correct enclosures and supplies at a reasonable price. Leopard Geckos are very economical pets, requiring a minimal amount of equipment and supplies to maintain them properly.

Leopard Geckos, at a pet or specialty shop, should be displayed in an enclosure that is a large enough for the geckos to have adequate hiding places to feel secure. It is important that the animals are never crowded. Crowding stresses out Leopard Geckos, possibly causing the gecko to stop eating, and producing an unhealthy animal. It is not advisable to purchase a Leopard Gecko from facilities that are not properly maintaining the animals.

THE INTERNET

The Internet is another place to search for a Leopard Gecko. Many well-known and respectable private dealers of Leopard Geckos have their own websites. Website addresses are usually listed in magazine advertisements, classified ad sections on major reptile websites, or are found by searching the Internet using the words, "Leopard Gecko", "*Eublepharis macularius*", or "Leopard Gecko dealers".

Occasionally, problems have occurred with unscrupulous

dealers. When dealing on the Internet with someone unknown, you assume they are honest and credible. However, being unable to visit their facilities or examine the Leopard Gecko, you must rely completely on the word of the dealer. Some people offering Leopard Geckos for sale on the Internet are not breeders but are simply buying and reselling animals. Many times they cannot give you the correct advice and information on proper setup, diet, and care.

Check various websites comparing Leopard Geckos being offered for sale, their prices, terms of sale, guarantee, and how the animals will be shipped. Also, ask if they will provide a photograph of the exact gecko you will be purchasing. If the seller is not the breeder, inquire who bred the Leopard Gecko, the approximate age, how it has been kept, and the diet. Most Leopard Gecko prices are fairly consistent and are usually within a certain range. Leopard Geckos are very reasonably priced, however, if the price seems too good to be true, then it's "buyer beware".

When purchasing a Leopard Gecko over the Internet, inquire as to exactly how the gecko will be shipped, the cost, and delivery time. Most legitimate breeders and dealers will properly pack Leopard Geckos to ensure live delivery. Ask if a "live delivery" is guaranteed and have the total cost stated in writing. You want your Leopard Gecko to be delivered safely in all types of weather. Leopard Geckos are usually shipped as Express Mail or by an overnight carrier with delivery to your door. Before committing to purchasing the Leopard Gecko, make sure the arrangements are clear and to your satisfaction.

If the seller gives you evasive answers, is unwilling to spend time answering your questions, or is just rude, look elsewhere to purchase your Leopard Gecko. These are usually deals that you will possible regret. There are plenty of reputable dealers offering quality healthy Leopard Geckos for sale on the Internet.

Chapter FOUR: HOUSING

Leopard Geckos are one of the easiest lizards to keep as a pet. Proper housing is important as the gecko must be comfortable within its captive environment. The captive habitat should simulate, as closely as possible, the natural habitat. The temperature, humidity, lighting, vegetation, and hiding areas should be similar to the hot and arid conditions in Afghanistan and Pakistan. Maintaining Leopard Geckos in an appropriate, comfortable environment is an important factor for long-term success of this species. A Leopard Gecko enclosure can be a simple setup or a more elaborate naturalistic vivarium.

Hatchlings and Sub-Adults

Leopard Gecko hatchlings and sub-adults should be housed in small, simple enclosures. Small enclosures are recommended so young geckos feel safe, secure, can readily find the food, and not became stressed. An ideal enclosure is a 10-gallon glass aquarium (20"l x 12"h x 12"w) fitted with a screen top. This is an excellent enclosure for up to three geckos. Aquariums are inexpensive, available in various sizes, and are easy to decorate for an attractive setup. Leopard Geckos don't climb or jump well, but screen tops prevent geckos from accidentally escaping, will keep out family pets and small children, and will eliminate the escape of insect prey.

The interior set-up for hatchling Leopard Geckos should be kept relatively simplistic. Paper towel is an excellent substrate to use when the geckos are small. A hide box, a shallow water dish, and a small dish for food, if feeding mealworms, should be added. If feeding crickets, the simplistic interior makes it easy for the geckos to search for and to capture their food.

It is very important to maintain a clean environment for hatchling Leopard Geckos for proper growth and health. Cleanliness is easily achieved using paper towel as a substrate, as they are inexpensive and easily replaced. Since Leopard Geckos normally defecate in the same area of the enclosure, cleanup is relatively easy and can be done daily, if necessary.

Some breeders, myself included, prefer using only paper towels as the substrate for hatchlings and sub-adults. However, other breeders use orchid bark, indoor/outdoor carpeting or calcium carbonate sand, such as T-Rex Bone Aid Calci-Sand®. Never use play sand as a substrate. Play sand is silica sand and Leopard Geckos are unable to digest it. Impaction or

This small enclosure offers climbing space, humidity, and easy access to food that are necessary in the first weeks of a Leopard Gecko's life. Photo by Robbie Hamper.

other serious medical problems may occur if the play sand is ingested. A critical component for proper bone growth and overall general health in Leopard Geckos is calcium. Leopard Geckos will possibly ingest play sand seeking calcium when sufficient amounts are lacking in their diets.

Calcium carbonate sand is digestible and generally considered safe to use for all ages of Leopard Geckos. However, when using calcium carbonate sand as the substrate, some reptile veterinarians recommend monitoring the geckos to make sure they are not ingesting the sand. This is more likely to occur with hatchling and sub-adult Leopard Geckos who are seeking calcium during their rapid growth. To prevent any possible problems, make sure that sufficient amounts of calcium are always available. Keep a small dish filled with calcium in the enclosure so that the Leopard Geckos have access to calcium all of the time.

When Leopard Geckos are approximately five months old up to adult size, add an additional hide box. Use a plastic container with a lid and fill it half-full with damp vermiculite. Make a hole in the lid, approximately 2" in diameter, so it is large enough for the Leopard Gecko to go in and out easily. The damp substrate will give the Leopard Gecko a cool retreat area as well as moisture which is needed to help the gecko shed its skin.

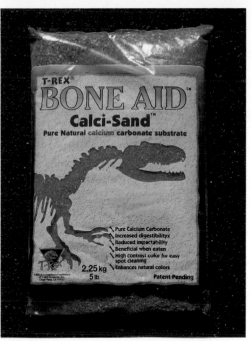

Calcium carbonate sand, which is available in a variety of colors, makes an attractive looking set-up in an aquarium. Photo by Sheri Ashley.

For housing larger groups of hatchlings or sub-adult Leopard Geckos, a 20-gallon long aquarium or a 28 qt. plastic Rubbermaid® container housed in a lidless, vertical rack system is recommended. Adequate hide boxes are advisable so the geckos do not become stressed. When several Leopard Geckos are housed together, it is essential to keep track of those geckos growing faster and becoming larger than the others. Geckos of similar sizes can be kept together, however, those growing faster than others must be removed into another enclosure. Sorting the sizes of multiple Leopard Geckos should be done on a weekly basis to ensure smaller geckos do not become stressed or denied adequate food.

Adults

Single adult Leopard Geckos can be easily housed in a 10-gallon aquarium with a screen top. Actually, this aquarium size is

A 28-quart Rubbermaid enclosure will adequately house 3-5 adult Leopard Geckos (either all females or one male and two to four females). Photo by Robbie Hamper.

adequate for a breeding pair of geckos or two females. For a breeding group, consisting of three to four females and one male, a 20-gallon long aquarium with a screen top or a 28-quart plastic Rubbermaid container, housed in a lidless rack system, is recommended. The recommended substrate for the enclosure whether for pets or for breeders is T-Rex Calci-Sand®, orchid bark, reptile carpeting, newspaper, or several layers of paper towels. In this setup, several hide boxes should be provided so the geckos have adequate hiding areas to feel safe and secure.

In this breeding situation, a laying box is needed and can be kept in the enclosure all the time. A closed plastic container, approximately 10"x 7"x 2 ½" works well. An opening should be cut in the lid large enough for the geckos to go in and out of easily. This container will serve not only as a laying box but as an additional hide box. It should be filled halfway with damp vermiculite.

The vermiculite should be kept damp at all times. This provides a cool retreat for the geckos, helps with shedding, and is

A 10-gallon aquarium with indoor / outdoor carpeting as a substrate is great for one or several subadult Leopard Geckos. Photo by Robbie Hamper.

an excellent environment in which the female can lay her eggs so they don't dry out. Another similar setup for breeding groups of Leopard Geckos can be established inside a 28 qt. plastic Rubbermaid® container on a shelf or in a rack system.

A larger water bowl should be used for adult geckos. At times, they will "lounge" in the water bowl either to cool down or to keep their skin moist while shedding.

It is critical that fresh, clean water is available at all times. The water should be changed on a daily basis so it does not become stagnant and contaminated with dead crickets, meal-worms, or fecal matter. Stagnant water can be a breeding area for bacteria or other pathogens which could be detrimental to the health of your Leopard Gecko.

Naturalistic Vivariums and Terrariums

For naturalistic vivaria, make sure you plan the setup

Two adult Leopard Geckos lounging in their 10-gallon terrarium with T-Rex calci-sand® as a substrate. Photo by Robbie Hamper.

carefully. Live plants, rocks, cork bark, drift wood, and even various lizards of different species can be established in this type of setup. However, when adding lizards, they must be similar in size, have similar habitat conditions, and be compatible. Naturalistic vivaria are not ideal setups for breeding projects but are great for display.

Naturalistic vivariums for adult Leopard Geckos can be setup using a calcium carbonate sand for the substrate such as T-Rex Bone Aid Calci-Sand®. Other substrates can be orchid bark or indoor / outdoor carpeting. de Vosjoli recommends using one part potting soil with two parts Calci-Sand® (de Vosjoli, Tremper, Viets, and Klingenberg, 1998). Vivarium and terrarium decor should be able to survive in the Leopard Geckos's dry, hot habitat of 85° to 90° F. Live plants such as succulent Philodendron (*Zamiaculcas zamiifolia*), Aloes, or Haworthias. Avoid succulents with spines as this will be detrimental to the health of the Leopard Geckos. If using live plants in your naturalistic setup, full-spectrum fluorescent lighting will suffice. Do not place your vivarium or terrarium by a window with sunlight for your plants. The sunlight shining on the glass enclosure can cause the interior to overheat, possibly killing your Leopard Gecko. There are many plastic plants, including a wide selection of life-like cacti, suitable to include in naturalistic setups. This is a safe but still realistic looking alternative to live plants. Other decor can include cork bark, driftwood, dried Cholla wood, rocks or anything that will be safe for your Leopard Gecko. If adding rocks or other items that can fall on your Leopard Gecko, make sure to secure them to the side of the enclosure or to each other, especially if you are stacking them or making a hiding cave. Silicone or epoxy glue both work well, but must be allowed to "cure" before your Leopard Gecko is placed inside the enclosure where the rocks or other items have been glued. Silicone and epoxy glues emit fumes during the curing process. Only use glues in well-ventilated areas.

Note: Never place two mature adult male Leopard Geckos together as they will not be compatible. Males are territorial and will become aggressive towards each other causing serious injury or death.

Temperature and Lighting

Since Leopard Geckos are cold-blooded and cannot make their own body heat, they must rely on heat from an outside source. Heat is needed for them to keep warm but is critical for them to digest their food. Too cool or too hot of a temperature will cause a loss of appetite, a weakened immune system, slower growth rate, and possible health problems.

Leopard Geckos should be kept at an optimum air temperature of 84° F to 88° F (29° C to 31° C) during the daytime and 74° F to 78° F (22° C to 25° C) during the nighttime. A 40-60 watt incandescent white or red light bulb, used as lighting over the screened top, is usually sufficient as the heat source over various sizes of aquarium enclosures. Since Leopard Geckos thermoregulate, place the light over one end of the enclosure. This creates a warmer and a cooler space in the same enclosure, giving the Leopard Gecko the option to decide when and where it will be most comfortable at any given time. Leopard Geckos are nocturnal, and therefore, do not require a UV light for calcium absorption, however, a UV-B-emitting florescent bulb can be used to create "daylight". It is advisable to give the geckos a day / night cycle to simulate conditions in nature. A red light bulb will allow geckos to be observed after dark when they are out searching for their food, but will not interrupt the day/night cycle. A timer can be used to produce this 12 hour day / night cycle.

A small heating pad, such as the T-Rex Cobra Heat Mat® or heat tape strips, can be placed under the aquarium on the warm side to give additional heat. Heat from the bottom of the enclosure will help Leopard Geckos digest their food. If you are using a rack or shelf system, heat tapes are placed in the back under the containers leaving the front of the container cooler. Heat tapes are controlled by rheostats and can be adjusted if the enclosure gets too cool or too warm. A thermometer placed at each end of the enclosure will indicate the temperature range on the cool and warm side. By knowing the temperatures in both the warm and cool areas, necessary adjustments can be made with the lighting so the gecko will be able to thermoregulate.

Caution: *Never use a hot rock as these can cause very serious burns to Leopard Geckos!*

Humidity

Even though in the wild Leopard Geckos come from dry, arid areas, the underground holes and crevices, where they spend a lot of time, are cool and somewhat humid. Humidity is important for proper shedding of the Leopard Gecko's skin. When the humidity level is too low, improper and incomplete shedding will occur. Patches of unshed skin can cause the new underlying skin to die and become necrotic. The unshed skin becomes a constricting band, cutting off circulation. This occurs more frequently on the toes, arms, legs, and around the eyes. This can lead to the possible injury or atrophy of the affected parts or, in extreme cases, cause an infection leading to death. An enclosure that is too high in humidity can lead to feeding problems and possible respiratory issues.

Maintenance

Cleanliness is extremely important to maintain healthy Leopard Geckos. All fecal matter and dead or uneaten food should be removed immediately. Leopard Geckos typically defecate in one particular area every time. Cleaning the fecal matter should routinely be done at least once a week to ensure a healthy environment. Unsanitary and dirty conditions will lead to unhealthy Leopard Geckos, causing them to stop eating which will lead to death. A clean environment will also prevent the attraction of ants or other insects that feed on this matter.

Once a month, it is recommended to empty and completely sanitize the enclosure with a mild bleach solution consisting of one part bleach to ten parts water (1:10). Thoroughly rinse the enclosure before returning the Leopard Geckos back into their cleaned habitat. If plastic hide boxes have been used, these also should be cleaned and sanitized. However, if cork bark, twigs, branches or foliage are used to accessorize, only rinse these off in warm tap water and never with the bleach solution.

Mixing Species

Many times, people are tempted to house different species together in the same enclosures. Requirements such as heat, light, moisture, and diet are usually species-specific with each individual gecko or reptile species. Certain gecko species can become dominant, territorial, and/or aggressive towards each other. If the specific needs are not met for each species, stress or other health-related problems can occur. Stress can lead to loss of appetite, outbreak of diseases, or aggression. Stress-related problems could result in injury or death of the geckos in a habitat with "mixed" species. Research and knowledge of species that will co-habitate is essential before housing them together.

Quarantine

A quarantine period of approximately 30 to 60 days is always advisable for new Leopard Geckos you are adding to your existing collection. Quarantined Leopard Geckos should be in a separate area from other Leopard Geckos or other reptiles. Even if your new Leopard Geckos are captive bred and appear healthy, they should be isolated as a precaution.

Geckos can develop a resistance to certain parasites and pathogenic germs that they have co-existed with previously. However, placing a gecko into a new environment can cause stress which may weaken its immune system and make the gecko susceptible to new and different parasites or pathogenic germs. A reptile veterinarian can check fecal samples if there is a suspected health problem. During this quarantine time, you can observe how your gecko is adapting to its new environment and make sure it is acting healthy and alert.

Maintenance of quarantined animals should be done after finishing with your existing collection. This will help to lower the risk of possible cross-contamination of diseases.

When the quarantine time has ended and the new Leopard Gecko or geckos are established, eating well, and appear healthy, they can then be placed into a permanent home and introduced to the existing collection.

Chapter FIVE: DIET

Little Leopard Gecko with a big appettite. A keeper must make sure that prey items are the appropriate size for their gecko. Photo by Robbie Hamper.

Leopard Geckos are low-maintenance lizards, especially in the area of their diet and nutritional requirements. The Leopard Gecko's natural habitat consists of rocky desert, sparse grassland and brush, and a minimal amount of moisture. Leopard Geckos are nocturnal hunters of live prey and feed on worms, grubs, and insects in the wild.

Food and Feeding

Leopard Geckos are carnivorous, feeding on live, moving prey. Their diet does not consist of any vegetables or fruits. The first Leopard Geckos in captivity were fed mealworms (*Tenebrio molitor*) as commercially raised crickets were not available as they are now. With advancements in nutrition and knowledge for maintaining healthy geckos, herpetoculturists now "gut-load" crickets and mealworms approximately 12 hours before offering them to the geckos. "Gut-loading" means feeding the crickets and mealworms a very healthy diet which consists of various grains such as wheat, bran, oats, or a mixed-grain baby cereal. T-Rex Leopard Gecko Dust® is a very good cricket "gut-loading" product used by many Leopard Gecko breeders. An excellent, inexpensive diet

Crickets should be fed assorted vegetables and fruit and a high-quality commercial diet just before feeding them to Leopard Geckos. Photo by Sheri Ashley.

is Layena®, a chicken feed found at farm supply stores. In addition to the grains, mealworms can be fed small pieces of cantaloupe, carrot, apple, oranges, pear, and other fruits or vegetables. Crickets should be fed dark green leafy vegetables such as kale, romaine, red or green-leaf lettuce, and mustard and collard greens. Crickets will also get their water supplement through the greens, carrots, and oranges.

Crickets or mealworms are both nutritional prey items for Leopard Geckos. Wax-worms can be offered as an occasional treat. Wax-worms have a high fat content with little nutritional value for geckos. However, if a gecko has stopped eating because of stress or illness, wax-worms are a good choice to try as Leopard Geckos are attracted to their wiggling and will eat them like "candy".

Some Leopard Gecko owners will offer newborn mice ("pinkies") as a supplemental food item. Most major breeders do not feed their Leopard Geckos "pinkies" since this probably is not part of their natural diet in the wild and nutritional requirements

"Shake-n-Bake" way of dusting crickets. Photo by Robbie Hamper.

can be met with the crickets and mealworms. However, "pinkies" are a good source of additional protein.

Crickets should be dusted with T-Rex 2:0 Calcium / No Phosphorus® or another calcium powder and multivitamin/mineral mixture just before feeding them to your Leopard Geckos. The crickets can be dusted with the powder supplement by the "shake-n-bake" method in a plastic container. I recommend that keepers dust the crickets each time they feed. After feeding crickets to your geckos, remove any uneaten crickets the following day. Crickets are capable of irritating Leopard Geckos to the point of causing the gecko to become stressed.

Mealworms also need the calcium and multivitamin/mineral supplement added before feeding them to the Leopard Geckos. The powder supplement should be sprinkled over the top of the mealworms after they have been placed into a shallow feeding dish in the gecko's enclosure. Mealworms tend to become smothered and die quickly if the "shake-n-bake" method is used to coat them.

Leopard Gecko breeders do not seem to have a preference of prey item for their geckos. Some breeders feed only mealworms, some feed only crickets, and some alternate the diet using both mealworms and crickets. In these different situations, there seems to be no difference in the growth rate, body size, or health of the geckos. The determining factor when deciding whether to use crickets or mealworms as the feeder food is usually the availability, ease of maintenance, and cost.

To ensure a Leopard Gecko is getting enough calcium at all times, fill a small lid with T-Rex 2:0 Calcium / No Phosphorus® or another similar calcium supplement and leave it in the enclosure. Leopard Geckos will be able to lick the calcium when they feel it is needed for their health. The extra calcium supplement should be included in the cages of the Leopard Geckos regardless of their age or size.

Hatchlings and Juveniles

Hatchling Leopard Geckos will usually start eating three to five days after hatching. Since Leopard Geckos hatch from eggs, absorption of the egg yolk continues for several days providing the nourishment needed for the gecko during this time. Leopard Geckos will shed for the first time before they start to eat. This will occur within the first few days but since they eat the shed skin, this process may not be observed. Hatchling Leopard Geckos should have food offered to them soon after the first shed.

Hatchling geckos can be started out on small meal worms approximately ½" in length, or small crickets, approximately ¼" to ½" size. Three to five crickets can be offered for each hatchling gecko. To decide on the cricket size for younger Leopard Geckos, just look at the length from the eye to the nostril. This will be the proper cricket size. The cricket should be smaller than the Leopard Gecko's mouth and the gecko should be able to easily catch and swallow the cricket.

If feeding mealworms, a shallow food bowl should be added to the Leopard Gecko enclosure. Keep it filled with enough mealworms so the gecko has plenty of food at all times. A hatchling will only eat two or three mealworms at each feeding but the mealworms will be available if it needs to eat more often.

I recommend feeding hatchling geckos on a regular daily basis. They are active, grow fast, and need plenty of nourishment. Old, inactive mealworms and crickets should be replaced every day with fresh ones. Leopard Geckos need

Time to chow down. A shoebox enclosure is a sufficient size for one sub-adult gecko. Photo by Robbie Hamper.

active food to attract their attention. Since Leopard Geckos are hunters, they will stalk and attack their food. It is recommended to feed them during the early evening.

As the Leopard Gecko grows into a juvenile, the crickets and mealworms offered should be larger. Juveniles should still be fed on a daily schedule but will do well if a keeper decides to feed on an alternate day schedule. Observation of your Leopard Geckos will give you an indication of how much food they consume and how often they need to be fed.

Adults

Adults can be maintained on the same diet as the hatchlings and juveniles. Adults can be fed full-sized crickets and mealworms. They will normally eat between five and seven crickets at each feeding. It is important for adult breeders to have sufficient calcium at all times, especially the female, so she remains healthy and is capable of producing properly calcified eggs.

Calcium and Multivitamins

A few of the recommended supplemental products are:

Calcium supplements:
T-Rex 2:0 Calcium / No Phosphorus®
Rep-Cal® (Phosphorus-free) – Calcium with Vitamin D3
NEKTON-REP®
Osteoform®

Multivitamins:
T-Rex Cricket Calcium Plus®
Rep-Cal® Herptivite®
Vionate®

Combinations:
Miner-All®
Zoo-Med Reptivite®

Note: It is highly recommended that only commercially raised crickets be used to feed your reptiles. Live crickets or other prey from outside could possibly have come in contact with pesticides or other chemicals that would be detrimental to the health of your Leopard Gecko. In addition, wild crickets are known to be carriers of a variety of internal parasitic worms.

Chapter SIX: BREEDING

Albino male preparing to mate with a High Yellow Leopard Gecko. Photo by Robbie Hamper.

Leopard Geckos are known to be the "perfect" pet to raise and breed in captivity. They are low-maintenance, hardy, and prolific breeders. When Leopard Geckos first emerged in the pet trade, imported from the wild, they were dull in color and fairly unattractive. Now, through selective breeding, Leopard Geckos are found in a multitude of colors, patterns, designs and mutations. The new characteristics now being produced are commonly referred to as morphs. Spontaneous mutations have produced leucistics, or pattern-less, albinos, and blizzards. With thousands of Leopard Geckos being produced each year, many more new and interesting morphs and mutations are expected to be produced in the future. Breeding Leopard Geckos offers an exciting challenge for both beginning and advanced breeders.

Breeding projects can range from producing small or large quantities of Leopard Geckos to the more specialized projects of producing new and exciting morphs. Before deciding the direction of your breeding program, remember that to have a successful program, it will probably involve extra time and investing extra money. These extra expenses are for purchasing quality animals, housing, feeding, general care and maintenance, and the extra burden of the new offspring.

Sexing

When starting a Leopard Gecko breeding project, the first priority is to make sure the breeding pair consists of an adult male and an adult female. Sexual dimorphism exists between males and females, but often it is difficult to determine the sex of a young gecko by only looking at the structure of the body. As adults, males tend to be slightly more heavy- bodied with a slightly broader head and thicker neck. To truly determine the sex of a Leopard Gecko, you must look at the underside of the gecko at the base of the tail and vent opening.

Leopard Geckos, younger than three to four months old, are difficult to visually sex. Leopard Geckos can be sexed as hatchlings using a 10x magnifying scope to look for the femoral or pre-anal pores, however, this is very difficult and requires patience, practice, and experience to accomplish this technique.

As males and females mature, it is relatively easy to deter- mine the difference. Male Leopard Geckos develop an external pair of hemipenal bulges located at the base of the tail, just behind vent. Males also develop enlarged pre-anal pores in an inverted V-shaped row of scales located just in front of the vent. In mature males, pre-anal pores often secrete a substance that appears waxy and can be seen visually.

Female Leopard Geckos do not have the external budges seen in the males. The area directly behind the vent is relatively smooth looking. Females have the V-shaped row of scales, however, only small pits are developed in the pre-anal area just in front of the vent.

Sexual maturity of Leopard Geckos occurs between eight

Female (left) and Male (right) anatomy. Note V-shaped pre-anal pores and hemipenal bulges of the male. Photo by Robbie Hamper.

and nine months of age.

Breeding is possible at this age but it is recommended to not start breeding Leopard Geckos until they are twelve months old with females being at least 50 to 55 grams. Overall growth in length and bone structure is achieved by this time. Breeding females too young can cause stress, calcium loss, and health problems. Female Leopard Geckos, when they have reached full size and maturity before breeding, will tend to produce more clutches with a higher percentage of viable eggs.

Breeding

Leopard Geckos, when healthy and sexually mature, will automatically breed without provocation, special attention or conditions other than the previously described proper habitat. As first time breeders, the geckos will usually mate upon being introduced to each other at any time of the year. Leopard Geckos that have been previously bred, are probably already on a breeding cycle. Leopard Geckos will breed as single pairs or in a group consisting of one male with several females. In a breeding group, check to make absolutely sure there is one male and only one male. More than one male in a group will result in aggressiveness towards each other, possibly resulting in injuries and, quite often, death. When breeding Leopard Geckos in a group, a recommended optimal ratio would consist of one male with three to five females. An enclosure such as a 28 quart Rubbermaid® tub or a 20-gallon long aquarium is a good size. More than four or five females in the enclosure could lead to overcrowding, the male possibly not mating with all of the females, or stress, all resulting in low egg production or infertile eggs.

During breeding, males tend to be extremely aggressive toward the female. He will typically rapidly tap his tail, making a noise which announces to the female that he is ready to breed. The male will begin to chase the female around the enclosure, and when he catches her, he will proceed to mount her from behind for copulation. During mating, males will excessively bite the top of the female's head. This is normal breeding behavior for Leopard Geckos during mating. If the bite breaks the skin of the female causing an open wound, the area should be cleaned with water and treated with an antibiotic such as Neosporin® or Polysporin®. It is not uncommon for the female's tail to become detached during breeding. This is something that occasionally happens during breeding. If the female is injured during mating, she should be immediately removed and treated daily with an antibiotic until the wound heals. The female can then be reintroduced into the enclosure for egg-laying and further breeding.

Inside the breeding enclosure, place an egg-laying container with a lid, approximately 10" x 7" x 2 ½" in size. Cut a 2" diameter hole in the lid close to one of the corners. The size of the hole must be large enough for the female to easily crawl inside to lay her eggs. Fill the egg-laying container with a loose substrate that can be kept damp all the time. Vermiculite is the substrate preferred by most professional breeders. It is a safe, clean substrate for Leopard Geckos and the eggs. The substrate should be about 1 ½" to 2" deep, loose in texture, and kept moist all of the time.

This allows the female to easily dig a hole, lay her eggs, and cover them with the substrate.

Leopard Gecko females, during their breeding season, need an abundant amount of calcium supplemented with vitamins and minerals. Female Leopard Geckos not only need calcium for their health, but also to ensure that the eggs will calcify properly. Sufficient food, coated with the

Always include a small dish of calcium in the Leopard Gecko enclosure. Photo by Robbie Hamper.

calcium, vitamin/mineral supplement, should be available, ideally, on a daily basis or at least, every other day. Additionally, small separate bowls filled with the vitamin/mineral supplement should be placed in the enclosure so the Leopard Geckos will have access to it at all times.

If the Leopard Geckos have previously bred, then a resting period is recommended to give the geckos time to recuperate and to regain weight and energy. This is especially important for the females who have endured stress from the male mating with her and egg production. Three to four months is usually sufficient time for the Leopards Geckos to become healthy and reach an optimal body weight to be ready for the next breeding season.

Some breeders also suggest a cooling down and cycling period of four to eight weeks after the "rest period" prior to

Eggs can be seen through the transparent skin of the female Leopard Gecko. Photo by Robbie Hamper.

breeding. This cooling period tends to imitate the seasonal temperature change of the natural habitat of Leopard Geckos and is believed to initiate more natural breeding behavior. For the cooling down period, temperatures can be in the range of 72° F to 76° F (22° C - 24° C) for daytime and 65° F (18° C) for nighttime. Feeding is suspended during this time but a water bowl should still be provided. Many breeders provide a rest period, but not the cooling down period, and still have successful breeding seasons.

The group breeding method is efficient and economical, but it is critical to monitor the health conditions of all Leopard Geckos carefully. Some females can become dominant and territorial over the other females. If any females appear thin, weak, and unhealthy, this is usually evidence that they are not competing well for food, are being harassed by the dominant female, are fighting, or are being over bred by the male. Any female appearing to have health problems should be separated immediately and given special attention before reintroducing her back into the breeding group. Males will also stop eating, become thin and unhealthy as a result of stress or over-breeding the females. The thin male should be removed and allowed to recover before returning him to the breeding enclosure. To help male and female Leopard Geckos regain their weight quicker during breeding season, feeding a small "pinkie" mouse, dusted with calcium, is recommended as a nutritional supplemental food.

If your breeding project is selectively breeding under controlled conditions to possibly develop new morphs, then the females should be housed individually and introduced to the male in his enclosure, one at a time. The male can also be introduced to each individual female's enclosure. He should remain with the female for approximately three days. However, breeding usually occurs the first day. Breeding is usually very successful. Accurate breeding records can be kept for each female as to when she was bred, when her eggs were laid, and, if and when the eggs hatch. If the female does not produce eggs or fertile eggs, she should be reintroduced to the male again. According to some literature, Leopard Geckos can retain sperm successfully up to a year after the initial copulation. However, to be sure of successful breeding, most breeders continue breeding the females on a regular schedule.

Breeding Season

Breeding season for captive Leopard Geckos usually extends from January to August or September. Many factors will determine the breeding cycle for Leopard Geckos. Some geckos will start early in the season and will cease breeding early while others will start breeding late in the season and continue into the fall. Some breeders, using controlled conditions, are able to cycle their Leopard Geckos to breed year round.

Record Keeping

Record keeping is important for an organized breeding program. Good record keeping allows tracking of individual breeding Leopard Geckos or a whole breeding group. Records are kept to indicate the origin and age of the geckos, date the breeding groups were set up, laying dates and number of viable and non-viable eggs produced by each female, and hatch rate of the eggs. Monitoring annual egg production and the hatch rate of these eggs will indicate if the breeding pairs or breeding groups are successfully mating to produce viable eggs. If your records indicate Leopard Gecko pairs or groups are not breeding successfully or breeding but only producing minimal viable eggs, various factors should be considered as the cause.

Some possible causes of breeding problems:

1. Health of the Leopard Geckos is not optimal for breeding. Some causes could be possible illness, nutritional requirements not met, unhealthy breeding enclosure, or overcrowding.

2. The Leopard Geckos are sexually immature and too young or small for breeding.

3. Female Leopard Geckos are too old and past their prime for production. Experienced Leopard Gecko breeders recommend retiring the females after 4-5 years and replacing them with young adult females.

4. Male Leopard Geckos can be infertile and lack ability to fertilize the eggs. If egg production is low or eggs are infertile, try replacing the male. Keep a record of egg production with the new male.

5. The Leopard Geckos are not comfortable in their habitat or enclosure.

6. Breeding pairs and groups are incorrectly sexed. Make sure there is only one male and not all females.

Breeding Leopard Geckos can be a great learning experience. Breeding them presents many challenges, with positive and negative results, but most Leopard Gecko breeders find it fun, interesting, educational, and rewarding.

Chapter SEVEN: EGGS AND INCUBATION

A simple setup for breeding Leopard Geckos includes a shelter, a food dish, a shallow water dish, and a laying box filled with vermiculite. Photo by Robbie Hamper.

Leopard Geckos will typically breed for seven or eight months during the breeding season. During this time, the female can lay six to eight clutches, usually consisting of two eggs in each clutch. The number of clutches a female will lay usually depends upon her age at the time of breeding. "First timers" and young females will not be as prolific as older, more mature females.

Incubation Substrate

For Leopard Gecko eggs, there are two substrates recommended to use as the medium in the egg incubation container. One is vermiculite, a type of heat-treated mica with no organic compounds that absorbs and holds moisture, or perlite, a naturally occurring volcanic glass made up of siliceous rock that traps and holds moisture. Both are sold at garden supply centers.

This female Leopard Gecko has just finished laying her two eggs but has not yet covered them up with the vermiculite. Photo by Robbie Hamper.

The dry substrate, whether vermiculite or perlite, or a mixture of the two, should be mixed thoroughly with distilled or purified water in correct proportions before placing it into the egg incubator container. The correct ratio of dry substrate to water is important so an even level of moisture and humidity is maintained at all times. Too much moisture could cause the eggs to mold and too little moisture could cause the eggs to dry out.

Breeders using vermiculite usually recommend 1:1 ratio by weight using a digital scale. A 1:1 ratio is: 1 part dry substrate to 1 part water. Breeders using perlite usually recommend a slightly different ratio with less water – typically a ratio of 1:0.8 or so.

The mixture of substrate and water by weight is done with the egg incubator container on digital scales. Weigh the container with about 2" to 3" of the substrate (if your scales do not tare out, you must first weigh the container, then subtract the container weight from the total weight of the container and the substrate before adding water). Add the water slowly until the scales reflect the correct amount of water and substrate in the 1:1 or 1:0.8 ratio.

When mixing the dry substrate and water without digital scales, determining the water content must be done by feel or by guesswork. Add the water slowly and mix frequently until the substrate "feels" damp but not overly wet. Let the substrate set and recheck 24 hours later. If the substrate feels too dry, slowly add a little more water. If too damp, add more substrate and recheck again in 24 hours.

Incubation Container

Incubation containers can be of various sizes and shapes depending upon your anticipated egg production and type of incubation. Rubbermaid® or Sterilite® plastic shoebox containers with lids can hold up to 48 eggs (6 across and 8 down) or Rubbermaid's® 24 oz rectanglular "Servin' Savers" can hold up to 20 eggs (4 across and 5 down). Both containers are practical, inexpensive, easy to clean and sterilize, and fit conveniently into commercial or homemade incubators. If an incubator is not an option and the incubation is done on a shelf, the shoebox and "Servin' Savers" will stack neatly, making the most of the space.

Some breeders make small air holes for ventilation in the egg incubation containers and others do not. Either method is equally effective. If you decide to use air ventilation holes, place one or two holes in opposite corners of the container, approximately 3/4" down from the top edge. These ventilation holes should be small (approximately 1/8") so the eggs or substrate will not dry out and the humidity level in the egg incubation container will remain high. A soldering iron or drill can be used to make the small holes.

Even though the container has air holes for air ventilation, it is still necessary to remove the lid frequently for total air exchange. Be sure to replace the lid securely. If you are using an incubation container without air holes, it is very important to make sure the lid fits tightly and, at least once a week, remove the lid briefly for complete air exchange, replacing the lid tightly.

The egg incubation container, with the moistened substrate, should be set up several days before the eggs are placed inside. This allows time for the dry substrate to evenly absorb the water and for you to monitor the substrate, moisture, and humidity in the container to make sure it is not too damp or too dry.

Eggs

Female Leopard Geckos will normally lay two eggs approximately 21 to 28 day after successful mating occurs. It is not unusual for young or first time breeders to lay one egg. Starting about 2 weeks after the breeders have been placed together, the egg-laying container should be checked daily to make sure the moisture content of the substrate is correct and to check for eggs that have possibly been laid.

After the female Leopard Gecko lays her eggs in the container, she will cover them with the substrate. Leopard geckos usually will lay the eggs at one end of the container, however, always look through all the substrate thoroughly. If eggs are found outside the egg-laying container, it usually indicates the substrate moisture is too dry inside the egg-laying container. A female may even lay her eggs in the water dish as she seeks the needed moisture for her eggs. Eggs found in the water dish will be very soft and puffy. However, don't throw these eggs away! Remove them from the water dish and place them on a paper towel to dry out. When the eggshell becomes harder, place the eggs in the incubation container. If these eggs are in the water dish too long, they will not hatch, but many times, they are still viable and will hatch.

Healthy Leopard Gecko eggs are slightly soft when laid but firm up quickly, developing a leathery, semi-hard shell. Fertile and viable eggs with plenty of calcium in the shell will become chalky white in appearance. The eggs will be approximately ¾" to 1" (2.0 cm to 2.5 cm) in length and weigh about 2 grams each. Infertile eggs are often smaller in size, remain soft, feel sticky, and do not develop the chalky white appearance. When the eggs are fertile, and before the egg becomes firm, sometimes a slight pinkish area can be seen through the shell of the egg. This usually indicates a fertile egg with embryonic development beginning.

If the eggs look discolored, slightly dented, or infertile, do not discard them as they may still produce healthy Leopard Geckos. These eggs should be placed in a separate section of the egg incubation container or a completely different container so they can be monitored. If the eggs turn dark, smell badly and look moldy, or completely collapsed, then discard them as they will not hatch.

Egg setup

Carefully remove the eggs as soon as possible after the female has laid them in the egg-laying container. Before removing the eggs and placing them into the prepared incubation container, gently mark the top with an X using an extra fine Sharpie® or other pen.

Try not to shake or jostle the eggs when moving them to the egg incubation container. The eggs should be positioned in the egg incubation container the same way as the female laid them in the egg-laying container. Once embryos start to develop, moving the eggs around could cause the embryo to literally drown in the fluids inside the egg.

In the egg incubation container, which has been previously prepared, make a depression in the substrate with your finger for each individual egg. Leave a space between each egg, placing them with the X on top and approximately 1" apart. This allows room for proper air flow and circulation around each egg and space for the eggs to expand properly as the embryo grows inside. Some breeders completely cover the eggs with the substrate while others leave the eggs exposed on top and place a small amount of substrate around the eggs to keep them from moving out of their position.

During the incubation duration, remove the lid frequently, (at least once a week if no air holes have been placed in the egg incubation container) allowing for fresh air to flow into the container for ventilation. This lets you inspect the eggs and monitor the moisture content of the substrate. Check for eggs that have become dried up, moldy, or infertile. Remove these eggs as they are bad and will not hatch. After each inspection, record the

A typical setup for incubating Leopard Gecko eggs on damp vermiculite. Photo by Robbie Hamper.

incubation temperature, moisture level of the substrate, and the status of the eggs. These records can be useful for tracking the breeding and hatch rate success of a breeding group or an individual pair of Leopard Geckos.

TSD or Temperature-Dependent Sexual Determination

Temperature-dependent sexual determination (TSD) means the sex of the animal is determined by the egg incubation temperature and not by chromosomes at the time of fertilization. TSD is a unique, well-documented phenomenon occurring in nature with turtles, crocodilians, and many lizards. Leopard Geckos are part of this group of reptiles whose egg hatching temperatures determine the sex of the hatchlings.

Leopard Geckos hatch at temperatures between 78° F to 92° F (24.5° C to 32.5° C). For Leopard Gecko eggs:

78° F to 82° F (24.5° C to 27° C) degrees will produce a high probability of females.

83° F to 88° F (27.5° C to 30.5° C) degrees will produce a mixture of both females and males.

89° F to 92° F (31° C to 32.5° C) degrees will produce a high probability of males.

These temperatures are not fool proof, but many Leopard Gecko breeders have used these temperature guidelines for many years with reliable results for the production of males or females for their specific requirements.

Incubation Time and Temperature

Incubation time for Leopard Geckos ranges from 45 to 70 days, depending upon the incubation temperature or other factors unknown. The hatch time is dependent upon the temperature. At a lower temperature, Leopard Geckos take more time to develop requiring a longer time before hatching. At a higher temperature, Leopard Geckos develop faster, requiring less time to hatch. However, at the higher temperature, there is a greater risk of

An inexpensive commercial incubator can be excellent for successfully hatching Leopard Geckos. Photo by Robbie Hamper.

egg mortality. The temperature must stay below the critical peak point of 95° F (34° C).

Incubation – Incubator or Shelf

The Hove-Bator Reptile® incubator, Model #1602R, is recommended for smaller breeding projects. The Turbo Fan model must not be used as it generates too much heat, never going below the critical 95° F. An accurate thermometer is needed to be able to do precise calibrations for specific male and female temperatures, or the temperature for hatching both sexes. A recommended thermometer is the Taylor Thermo-Hygro®, Model 5368. (Albey, pers. com.).

Several days before the projected date for the female Leopard Gecko to lay her eggs, set up the incubator or incubation area, along with the egg incubation container so everything will be ready for the eggs. Setting up the incubator or the area for shelf incubation with the prepared egg incubation containers early allows time to monitor the temperature and moisture. With the incubator, check to make sure the temperature is consistent and disperses evenly. Adjustments can be made to the incubator or to the substrate during this time.

Larger incubators are available from various dealers or commercial businesses found on the Internet. Functional but inexpensive incubators can easily be made with basic materials and equipment. There are a variety of plans to build your own incubator that can be found in reptile books, on the Internet, or by talking with other reptile breeders who have constructed incubators.

Many breeders do not use an incubator to hatch Leopard Gecko eggs. The egg incubation containers are placed on a shelf in an area where the environmental or ambient temperature remains around 85° F (28.5° C). At this temperature, Leopard Geckos will hatch out as both males and females. Temperature fluctuation of several degrees of 85° F will not be a problem if incubating for both sexes. However, to specifically produce males or females using the shelf method, the incubation area must be a more consistent temperature within the ranges previously mentioned.

Leopard Gecko eggs can be incubated successfully in the proper containers on a shelf in a warm room. Photo by Robbie Hamper.

Chapter EIGHT: HATCHLING CARE

A Super Hypo Tangerine Leopard Gecko enters the world. Photo by Craig Stewart of The Urban Gecko.

How exciting when the first baby Leopard Gecko finally hatches! After anxiously waiting for 45 to 60 days, a tiny Leopard Gecko's head emerges. Success has been achieved! Actually, this is only the beginning, as complete success is achieved when Leopard Gecko hatchlings are properly housed, fed, and maintained on a regular basis so they grown into healthy, mature adults.

Hatching

Clues on the outside of the egg reveal that the Leopard Gecko is about to hatch. Small droplets of moisture, or sweat, will appear on the outside of the shell. The egg will begin to shrink and partially collapses, looking like it has gone bad and will not hatch. However, the egg is still good and has a live baby Leopard Gecko inside getting ready to greet the world. Unique changes are beginning to take place inside the egg so the baby can hatch.

Exactly what triggers this hatching process in not completely understood. It is known that towards the end of the incubation period, the Leopard Gecko has grown so large inside the egg that little space is left. As the space decreases inside, so does the oxygen level, causing a build-up of carbon dioxide. Possibly hormones or certain enzymes signal the Leopard Gecko that it is time to hatch. The Leopard Gecko is forced out of its safe, warm environment. The actual hatching process begins with the pipping of the tough egg shell.

"Egg Tooth" and Pipping

Leopard Geckos, similar to other reptile species, temporarily develop a calcareous tip on the end of their snout. This is called an "egg tooth". Leopard Geckos use the "egg tooth" to make longitudinal slits in the shell. While still inside, the baby Leopard Gecko will enlarge the slits using its head and legs. When the slits are opened wide enough, the head will emerge.

Some Leopard Geckos will remain in this position for several hours before completely emerging. With only the head out, Leopard Geckos will absorb the remaining yolk sac while resting and gaining strength to push completely out of the egg. While some geckos take time to hatch, others emerge quite quickly, immediately running around. Within a day or two, the "egg tooth" will fall off. It has served its purpose to slit the egg shell and is no longer needed.

Occasionally, a baby Leopard Gecko will emerge from the egg with the yolk sac not completely absorbed. Special care must be taken until absorption is completed. Carefully remove the hatchling Leopard Gecko from the egg incubation container and place it into a small enclosure, such as a deli cup, that is deep enough so the Leopard Gecko cannot climb out. The hatchling should be placed on a moist paper towel inside the enclosure and kept warm. Make sure the towel stays moist all the time so the yolk sac and hatchling do not dry out. If the yolk sac membrane is

These hatchling Leopard Geckos will soon be removed from their incubation container and into more permanent housing. Photo by Albey Scholl of Albey's "Too Cool" Reptiles.

still attached to the inside of the shell, do NOT try to detach the membrane from the shell. Remove the eggshell and hatchling together and place into the special moist, warm enclosure.

The small container must be kept clean during the time the Leopard Gecko is still absorbing the yolk sac. The paper towel should be changed daily to prevent the possibility of contamination. It is also important to check to make sure the Leopard Gecko is kept warm. The hatchling Leopard Gecko should not be disturbed during this time.

When the yolk sac appears to be completely absorbed, the membrane probably has already dried up and detached. Yolk sac absorption usually occurs within 1-3 days. After the absorption is completed, the Leopard Gecko can be transferred to an enclosure suitable for hatchlings.

Hatchlings

Newborn Leopard Geckos usually hatch out between 2 ½ " to 3 ½" (6.5 cm to 8 cm) in length and weighing approximately 1.5

to 2.0 grams. The size and weight of hatchling Leopard Geckos is dependent upon factors such as genetics of parents, size of the egg and yolk sac providing nutrients before hatching, incubation temperature, deformities, and other unknowns. Baby Leopard Geckos will shed within 24 hours of hatching. They will pull the skin off and eat it. A hatchling's shed skin is high in nutritional value, adding an additional source of food besides the yolk sac to sustain itself early in life.

If the baby Leopard Gecko does not completely shed its skin, it must be removed as soon as possible. Gently hold the gecko and thoroughly moisten the areas of dried shed skin with a spray of water. Once the skin is softened, it can be eased off with your fingers or carefully removed using tweezers.

Hatchling Leopard Geckos are tiny and cute, but fragile, becoming easily stressed. Do not handle or play with the babies as this will cause them to stress. When frightened, they arch their backs, rise up on their tiptoes, and emit a hissing sound. Overcrowding of hatchling Leopard Geckos and insufficient heat are other stress factors to avoid. If stressed, hatchlings will not eat, resulting in slow or no growth, colors will darken, and eventually, health problems or death.

Note: If you are considering purchasing a hatchling Leopard Gecko, it is advisable not to purchase one from a large, overcrowded group. They are usually displayed in an aquarium, under lights, and with no hiding areas provided. These hatchlings have already become stressed before you purchase the gecko. Setting up the hatchling gecko at home in its new habitat is an added stress, resulting in a high probability that the gecko will be slow starting to eat or will not even start to eat.

Hatchling Housing

Leopard Gecko hatchlings are fragile and need daily attention and care. They are best housed and raised in individual enclosures. For a single hatchling, a 10-gallon aquarium with a lid is ideal. There is plenty of room for a hide box, a shallow water dish, and a food dish, if feeding mealworms. Low wattage bulbs, such

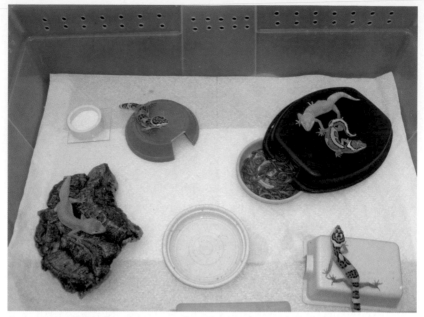

A roomy enclosure for raising a number of young Leopard Geckos. Note the addition of multiple shelters. Photo by Robbie Hamper.

as a 25- or 40-watt incandescent bulb placed over the top, will give the adequate heat of approximately 85° F for the young gecko. As the hatchling grows larger, it can still be housed in the same enclosure. There will be plenty of space for the gecko to move and roam around. Keep the bottom of the enclosure simple, using paper towel as the substrate. Paper towels can be changed frequently, providing a clean environment for the Leopard Gecko. The gecko can also find its food easily, especially if you are feeding it small crickets.

Hatchlings can also be individually housed in a lidless rack-type system using Rubbermaid® shoebox-sized enclosures. This rack system allows the enclosures to pull out like a drawer, giving a keeper easy access for servicing and maintenance. A lidless rack system will have strip heat tapes at the back and will provide heat underneath the boxes. Since the back section of the enclosures will remain warmer than the front, the Leopard Gecko is able to thermoregulate, or choose if it wants to be warmer or cooler. The temperature of the heat tapes is regulated with a rheostat. The temperature should be monitored frequently to be sure the warm section is approximately 85° F. Once the hatchling becomes a juvenile, it can be moved into a larger enclosure.

The Rubbermaid® shoebox containers are large enough for a shallow water dish, a food dish if feeding mealworms, and a hide box. These Rubbermaid® containers can also provide individual housing for adult Leopard Geckos. Many commercial breeders or dealers use this type of enclosure to ensure their Leopard Geckos are in prime condition for color, size and health.

For multiple housing of hatchling Leopard Geckos, a 10-gallon aquarium is functional as long as no more than three or four are housed together. Plenty of hide areas need to be provided to help prevent stress in this situation. If at any time, one or more are not growing as fast as the others or appears not to be gaining weight, then immediately separate them. Stronger, more dominant Leopard Geckos will prevent smaller, weaker ones from eating the food.

Larger groups of hatchling Leopard Geckos can be set up in large enclosures. An ideal size is a 28-qt Rubbermaid® container or large aquariums. Adequate water, food, hide boxes, and heat must be provided for larger setups.

Large-scale breeders usually use a lidless rack type system that facilitates the 28-qt. Rubbermaid® containers. Plastic tubs with cutouts, commercial shelters, or even layers of flat egg carton dividers can be used as hiding places for Leopard Geckos. A focused breeder can maintain approximately 20 hatchlings in this setup. However, it is advisable that a group of no more than 6 or 8 be grouped together. Overcrowding will easily cause stress and unsanitary conditions.

With group housing, it is essential to sort the geckos out by size every week to two weeks. Leopard Gecko hatchlings grow at various rates. Therefore, it is necessary to remove the geckos that have grown faster and are bigger than the others and place them into their own container. When a larger group of geckos are about 3 months old, they should be separated into groups of no more than 5 to 6 per container. When they are approximately 4 months old, they usually can be sexed visually, especially the males, by turning the gecko over and looking for the hemipenal bulges and the pre-anal pores. Once the males have been identified, watch them closely as they start to reach maturity (which can occur when they are between 7 to 9 months old).

A lidless rack-type system using 28-quart plastic Rubbermaid® containers. Photo by Robbie Hamper courtesy of Reptiles by Mack.

The males will become aggressive towards one other and must be separated out and placed into individual containers. Females can cohabitate without problems at any age.

A Hatchling's First Meals

Leopard Gecko hatchlings will not eat for 3-5 days after hatching. The absorbed yolk sac sustains them during this time. If feeding mealworms, a small dish of the worms can be placed inside the enclosure any time. This gives the Leopard Gecko the opportunity to start eating at any time. The smell, sight, and sound of the mealworms will get the geckos "tuned in" to where the food is located in the enclosure. If feeding small crickets, introduce a few on about the third day. If the Leopard Gecko does not eat them by the next day, remove the crickets and wait another day to offer the crickets again. Always remove excess crickets as they can easily stress the hatchling Leopard Gecko.

Hatchlings should have food available every day, either with a dish of small mealworms or small crickets. If feeding crickets, make sure the crickets are no larger than the length from the geckos' eyes to its mouth. By using this guide for cricket size, the cricket will always be smaller than the gecko's mouth and can be easily caught, eaten, and digested.

The crickets and mealworms should be dusted with calcium, and a mineral/vitamin supplement at each feeding. Hatchling Leopard Geckos grow rapidly during the first six months and need plenty of nutrients in their diet for proper bone and muscle growth. When purchasing a hatchling or sub-adult Leopard Gecko from a breeder or dealer, be sure to ask if the diet has been crickets, mealworms, or both. This is critical as Leopard Geckos that have been raised on mealworms will usually eat crickets. However, if Leopard Geckos are raised on crickets, they usually will refuse to eat mealworms. Regardless whether they were raised on mealworms or crickets, Leopard Geckos will always eat wax worms as a supplemental food and treat.

Myth: Leopard Geckos should not be fed mealworms as mealworms cannot be digested and will chew out from inside the stomach, killing the Leopard Gecko!

FALSE!!! Leopard Geckos, even as babies, have a strong lower jaw plus serrated teeth. This crushes the mealworm before it is swallowed and enters the stomach. Also, Leopard Geckos have digestive juices that adequately process mealworms.

Handling Hatchlings

Hatchling Leopard Geckos are relatively hardy, but being so tiny, they are still somewhat fragile. I highly recommend not to hold or play with hatchlings until they are larger and well-established. Leopard Gecko hatchlings are very agile and quick, and, if dropped, will quickly disappear. Handling a hatchling Leopard Gecko may cause undue stress, loss of its tail, and possible injury. When they are about 3 or 4 months old, a limited amount of handling can begin. Once they are a sub-adult or adult, handling is not a problem.

Chapter NINE: HEALTH and
DISEASES

Hatchlings with tail loss. Regeneration of a new tail begins immediately. Photo by
Robbie Hamper.

Leopard Geckos are one of the hardiest geckos in captivity. Living
for many years, and a loyal companion, Leopard Geckos have proven
themselves as an "ideal" pet. They are low-maintenance, have
relatively few health problems, and live an average of 5 to 7 years.

Following basic husbandry and using a good hygiene regimen with
proper nutritional maintenance, your Leopard Gecko will stay healthy
and thrive without medical problems. Preventing diseases and
disorders can easily be achieved by being aware of potential problems before they occur. Close observation of the Leopard Gecko's
habits, behaviors, and general condition, will prevent disorders and
diseases that could be detrimental to the health of the gecko.

Disorders

Some of the more common disorders are the following:

Gastroenteritis/Diarrhea

Normal stool appearance of Leopard Geckos should appear relatively dry and well-formed with a small white portion. Many times, the first indication of health problems or gastroenteritis in a Leopard Gecko is the presence of a watery stool or blood in the stool. The gecko has probably already started to lose weight, has a skinny tail, and is showing signs of overall anorexia. There may also be undigested cricket masses, the result of regurgitation or being passed with fecal material. The Leopard Gecko's color will darken and become dull in appearance. The Leopard Gecko will stop eating, become dehydrated and emaciated and possibly die.

Gastroenteritis is usually caused by a bacterial infection brought on by unsanitary conditions, improper maintenance, and neglect. It is extremely important to isolate and quarantine the ill Leopard Gecko from all other animals in your collection. Wash your hands thoroughly before touching any other animal and sanitize everything that has been inside the enclosure or in contact with the ill gecko. Gastroenteritis, caused by a bacterial infection, is contagious and can easily be spread by cross-contamination. Fecal cultures, taken by a qualified reptile veterinarian, may be needed to determine the exact diagnosis and treatment. Fecal cultures will also determine if the ill Leopard Gecko's problem is being caused by intestinal parasites such as coccidia or trichomonads.

If the diagnosed problem is trichomonads, the recommended treatment is with Flagyl® and Panacur® at the dosage prescribed by a reptile veterinarian.

Coccidia

Coccidia are small protozoan parasites in the intestinal lining are often the cause of gastrointestinal problems. The intestinal lining is invaded by the parasite, enabling reproduction to occur. Leopard Geckos infested with coccidia will stop eating, become dehydrated, lethargic, and anorexic. They may also develop a secondary bacterial infection. If a coccidia infection is suspected, a qualified reptile veterinarian should examine a fecal culture.

Coccidia parasites reproduce by means of oocysts, or eggs, which are released in fecal matter. The oocysts are the infective stage of coccidia. The oocysts must be ingested to invade another host to reproduce and complete their life cycle. When the fecal matter with the oocysts is deposited into the Leopard Gecko's enclosure, the gecko becomes the host again by re-infecting itself as well as any other Leopard Gecko in the enclosure.

Quarantine any sick Leopard Gecko immediately, completely away from other animals in your collection. Clean and sanitize the Leopard Gecko's enclosure at least once a day or more. Also, have clean, sanitized enclosures ready and available at all time so transferring the sick gecko can be done easily with less chance of cross-contamination. When working with your Leopard Geckos, wash your hands frequently, especially if you are going from one enclosure to another. A strict regimen of cleanliness will help prevent spreading any diseases to healthy geckos or other animals in your collection.

Metabolic Bone Disease (MBD)

Leopard Geckos are less apt to develop metabolic bone disease than other captive-hatched lizards. Metabolic bone disease is a nutritional deficiency caused by an insufficient amount of calcium and appropriate levels Vitamin D3 in the diet. Leopard Geckos with MBD become weak, the bones will become spongy, especially in the lower jaw, deformities appear in the forearms, legs, and spine, twitching or tremors can occur, and they will have a lack of appetite. Once signs of MBD appear, reversal of the condition is very difficult.

Preventive medicine is the key to avoiding MBD. It is important to routinely "dust" the crickets and mealworms with T-Rex 2:0 Calcium / No Phosphorus® or another high-quality calcium and a vitamin/mineral supplement at each feeding. In addition, place a shallow dish of calcium in the enclosure so the Leopard Geckos will have access to calcium at all times. Leopard Geckos will lick the calcium when needed. In the early, rapid growth stages, sufficient calcium, vitamin and mineral levels are critical factors for proper bone formation. Breeding female Leopard Geckos also need plenty of calcium and supplemental vitamins/minerals for proper calcification of the eggs.

Anorexia

Anorexia occurs as a result of stress, lack of cleanliness in the enclosure, nutritional

An unhealthy Leopard Gecko with a skinny tail next to a healthy gecko with a fat tail. Photo by Robbie Hamper.

disorders, diseases, or overall improper husbandry practices. Anorexic Leopard Geckos appear thin, develop an extremely thin tail, become weak and lethargic, stop eating, and will usually die.

Autotomy or Tail Loss

Autotomy is the dropping of the tail in geckos and other lizards. Tail loss is not uncommon and is a defense mechanism for geckos. Tail loss can happen with hatchlings if another gecko mistakenly nips the tail of another one. Tail loss is thus more likely to occur in overcrowded conditions. Breeding or fighting between two males can lead to tail loss. If a keeper grabs a gecko by the tail or handles it roughly, a gecko might drop its tail.

Leopard Geckos will regenerate their tails, however, they never look the same as the original tail. When autotomy occurs, the gecko has lost a large amount of its fat reserve. Special care and attention should be given to a Leopard Gecko that has lost its tail. It is best to remove the gecko into an enclosure by itself until the new tail has regenerated.

Dysecdysis

Dysecdysis, or shedding problems, occur when the old skin is not completely shed. This condition is usually the result of poor husbandry, lack of humidity or moisture in the enclosure, or poor nutrition. The incomplete shed skin will appear as dried patches on the head and eyes, body, toes, or tail. Leopard Geckos exhibiting shedding problems can have difficulty walking, develop eye problems, or noticeable constricting bands of skin around their limbs and digits. The dead shed skin must be removed as soon as possible. Moisten the area and gently ease off the skin using your fingers or tweezers. If not removed, infection or complete loss of constricted parts can occur.

Dystocia

Dystocia, or "egg-binding", occurs when a female Leopard Gecko retains her eggs, is unable to expel them, and eventually becomes "egg bound". The gravid female will become weak and lethargic, and will usually stop eating.

Dystocia usually occurs with a first-time breeding female that has not been provided a proper egg-laying container. Other contributing factors include eggs that are too large to pass through the oviduct and cloaca, nutritional factors, a weak or ill female, and other unknown problems with the female can lead to "egg-binding".

Infections

Infections occur frequently when shedding is incomplete. The most common infections are those to the digits when the dried, dead shed skin constricts the vascular system, resulting in the loss of the toes. Objects in the eye or improper shedding over the eye area will cause eye infections. Superficial scrapes and abrasions from fighting or breeding should be cleaned thoroughly with antibacterial soap or hydrogen peroxide and treated with Polysporin® or Neosporin® to prevent infections.

Stomatitis or Mouthrot

Leopard Geckos are not as prone to get stomatitis or mouthrot as are other reptiles. A noticeable swelling around the mouth area with a cheesy-like substance, or pus, inside are signs of mouthrot. With hydrogen peroxide or Betadine®, thoroughly clean the affected area, extracting all the cheesy pus. This should be done daily until the mouthrot clears up. A minimal amount of Neosporin® or Polysporin® can be applied to the area. The Leopard Gecko should be kept by itself on paper towel in a sanitized enclosure until the mouth is clear and healed.

Pneumonia

Pneumonia is a severe respiratory tract infection caused by bacteria in the lungs. Leopard Geckos very seldom get pneumonia, however, an environment where the temperature is too cool and humid can compromise the immune system of the gecko. This leads to low-resistance to diseases such as pneumonia. A Leopard Gecko with pneumonia will have mucus bubbles in the nostril area and will typically suffer from labored breathing. Increasing the temperature within the enclosure to the recommended 82° to 85° F will usually resolve the problem.

Sand Impactions

Intestinal impaction or rectal prolapses do not commonly occur. However, problems can occur if Leopard Geckos ingest particles of their substrate. Since Leopard Geckos are terrestrial geckos, there is always the possibility they could ingest small particles of the substrate that may adhere to the crickets or mealworms.

Never use play sand! Play sand is silica sand which is indigestible and may cause impactions or other serious medical problems. Even though play sand does not contain calcium, Leopard Geckos will ingest the sand if their diet is lacking calcium, a critical element for proper bone growth. When Leopard Geckos are supplied with adequate calcium in their diets, impactions tend not to occur.

Prolapse

Occasionally with Leopard Geckos, the male hemispenes (one or both), or the female reproductive tract, will prolapse. Try soaking the Leopard Gecko in a warm solution of dissolved sugar and water overnight. If this does not cause retraction of the prolapse, then seek help from a qualified reptile veterinarian.

Stress Factors

Bad husbandry practices cause the large majority of reptile health problems. Stress caused by bad husbandry is often the initial culprit initiating a deterioration of the Leopard Gecko's immune system. When the immune system becomes compromised, medical problems will usually be encountered.

Remember these proper husbandry guidelines:

1. Maintain Leopard Geckos in an atmosphere that is specific for their needs such as temperature, diet, size of enclosure, and humidity.

2. Refrain from overcrowding Leopard Geckos. They need plenty of secure hiding areas. Provide sufficient space for each gecko.

3. Only keep similarly sized Leopard Geckos together. Remove larger ones to prevent intimidation and dominance problems.

4. Breeding is very demanding and stressful for Leopard Geckos, especially females laying eggs. Close observation of the health of females during breeding and egg-laying time is critical.

5. Do not handle hatchling or juvenile Leopard Geckos since they are tiny and fragile. This will cause undo stress or injury to the gecko.

6. Maintain clean and sanitary conditions of the Leopard Geckos'

enclosures at all times. Unsanitary conditions are a cause of many serious health problems.

Preventive Medicine Suggestions

Preventing health issues before they arise is the key to maintaining healthy Leopard Geckos.

Keeping Leopard Geckos healthy and preventing the spread of pathogens or other diseases can be accomplished with a simple routine.

1. Fastidious hand washing is critical to the hobby of keeping Leopard Geckos as pets! Pathogens are microscopic organisms that cannot be detected visually. Pathogens can be transferred from an infected Leopard Gecko to a healthy gecko by cross-contamination from fecal material in the same enclosure or on the keeper's hands, fingers, or under the fingernails.

2. Sanitize all enclosures, containers, water bowls, hide boxes, or other items on a regular weekly schedule. Any items previously used by another Leopard Gecko or reptile must be thoroughly sanitized before reusing it for a new resident.

A mild bleach solution is recommended. The bleach solution should consist of 1 part bleach to 10 parts water. Rinse all items thoroughly after cleaning to remove any bleach residue. Other disinfectants are effective as long as they are non-toxic to Leopard Geckos.

Contaminated fecal material contains parasite eggs or bacteria that can remain viable for an extended length of time. A healthy Leopard Gecko may become infected by contact with any contaminated material that has not been properly sanitized.

3. Feed quality food, especially crickets. Buy from a reputable cricket supplier. Crickets should arrive from the supplier packed on new, clean egg cartons. Previously used egg cartons may contain pieces of eggshell or traces of chicken feces harboring pathogens. If crickets ingest anything that is contaminated, they may become

carriers, transferring pathogens to healthy Leopard Geckos. Remove uneaten crickets from the enclosure.

4. Good husbandry consists of keeping the enclosures of Leopard Geckos clean and sanitized at all times. Fecal material and excess or dead crickets or mealworms should be removed as soon as possible. Leopard Geckos can easily re-infect themselves when they eat their shed skin that has come in contact with contaminated feces left in the enclosure.

5. Quarantine any new or unhealthy Leopard Gecko immediately. The quarantine area should be in a separate area, away from any other Leopard Geckos or other animals in a collection. Quarantine new animals for at least 30-45 days. Unhealthy animals should be quarantined until they have recovered and have a clean bill of health. Handling quarantined Leopard Geckos must be done carefully and only in the quarantine area to prevent exposure and contamination of other animals. Thoroughly washing your hands with an antibacterial soap or mild beach solution is critical before leaving the quarantine area!

Remember:

A healthy Leopard Gecko is a happy gecko. A pet that is free from disease and nutritional disorders will be an enjoyable pet for many years, requiring only your love and attention. You are the keeper, caregiver, and guardian of this ideal reptile pet. You have accepted a great responsibility to provide a quality, healthy life for your pet, and in return your Leopard Gecko will always have a smile on its face!

THE FUTURE

During the last several years, the Leopard Gecko phenomenon has continued to excel to new heights with an explosion of unbelievable new colors, patterns, and mutations. This is just the beginning of what the future might hold for Leopard Geckos.

Leopard Geckos are uniquely specialized to survive in the wild. Since they are found in areas of harsh terrain with little change in environmental conditions for thousands of years, their physical adaptation has accommodated them to survive. Luckily, habitat destruction by man is not a threat at this time.

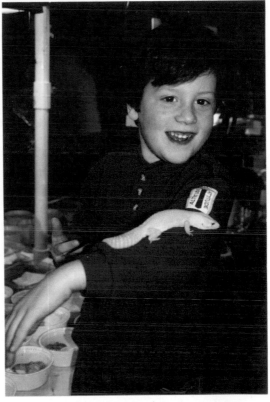

Leopard Geckos make ideal reptile pets for those willing to meet their simple needs with thoughtfulness and care. Photo by Robbie Hamper.

With the popularity of Leopard Geckos as reptile pets, their long-term survival in captivity should be safe and secure. Captive propagation of Leopard Geckos can be attributed to their low-maintenance, ease of breeding, and to the many dedicated and caring breeders. The delightful but humble Leopard Gecko has brought so much brightness and entertainment into our lives the last several years. The future now depends upon all of us, as owners, to do our part in the continued captive survival of Leopard Geckos. Feed your imagination with what might be possible for the future relating to colors, patterns and mutations. Others may try to discourage you and point you to more high-profile, high dollar animals for breeding projects, but don't let them define your goals, challenges, and ambitions.

Leopard Geckos don't ask for much other than the commitment of daily care and dedicated love from their owners. Don't ever let them down!

A quote attributed to Chief Seattle, of the Suquamish Tribe that I particularly like, says:

"What is man without the beast?
If all the beasts were gone,
Man would die from a great loneliness of spirit.
For whatever happens to the beasts,
Soon happens to man,
All things are connected."

Thank you for caring,

Robbie Hamper

THE AFRICAN FAT-TAILED GECKO

A beautiful Amelanistic African Fat-tailed Gecko and a heterozygous Fat-tailed Gecko. Photo by Ruben Lugo of Taino Reptiles.

African Fat-tailed Geckos, *Hemitheconyx caudicinctus*, are indigenous to Nigeria and Senegal, West Africa. Their habitat is in the hot, humid, rocky hillside areas. African Fat-tailed Geckos are nocturnal, roaming around and searching for food from early dusk to dawn. Their rich, chocolate coloration combined with darker brown banding, provides wonderful camouflage in this habitat, especially when searching for food. African Fat-tails are carnivores, and, in the wild, eat insects, such as grasshoppers, locusts, and crickets. Even though African Fat-tailed Geckos are still being imported, they are now being captive bred by many breeders. African Fat-tailed Geckos are gaining popularity with the introduction of beautiful new color morphs, such as peach, pale gray, leucistic, white striped, and the amelanistic. Many of these "designer" Fat-tails also exhibit bands of orange and salmon coloration in the tails, adding to their beauty. As more of these new morphs are becoming available, reptile hobbyists and herpetoculturists have found a new challenging direction to pursue.

The African Fat-tails Gecko, like the Leopard Gecko, belongs to the *Eublepharine* family of geckos which have moveable eyelids and lack sticky toe pads or lamellae. The African Fat-tail's scientific name, *Hemitheconyx caudicinctus*, means: *Hemi*, half or divided, *theconyx*, box claw or nail, and *caudicinctus*, ring-tailed. They range in size from 6" upwards to 10". Females tend to remain smaller in total length, head size, and thickness of the neck. Like Leopard Geckos, they are thick-bodied with short limbs and with a thick, robust tail. African Fat-tailed Geckos are nocturnal, sleeping during the daytime and becoming active at nighttime in their search for food. Having short limbs and an elongated body, enables them to easily slip between the crevices, cracks, and holes in their rocky habitat, escaping their predators.

During the daytime, African Fat-tails sleep in damp underground holes or burrows, staying cool during the hot African days. Like the Leopard Gecko, African Fat-tails also store excess fat in their tails. They rely on this fat reserve to survive when food is scarce or during hibernation.

African Fat-tailed Geckos shed their skin. When a Fat-tail "out-grows" its old skin, shedding occurs. When the old skin becomes loosened from the new skin underneath, the Fat-tail will pull the skin off with its mouth, then, proceed to swallow it completely. This process is called "ceratophagia" which means "horn-eating". Eating the old skin is probably a defense mechanism which means no trace or odor is left behind to alert a predator to their presence. The old skin also contains nutrients that may be beneficial to the survival of African Fat-tailed Gecko in its harsh habitat.

African Fat-tailed Geckos are charming, docile, and friendly, making them an ideal lizard for a pet. They are hardy, low-mainte-nance, usually don't bite, and live a relatively long time.

Although wild-caught African Fat-tails are still imported, it is highly advisable to purchase only those that are captive-hatched. Many imported specimens are stressed, dehydrated, diseased, parasitized, and emaciated. Imported African Fat-tails may look healthy when purchased, but, be aware, they may harbor flagellate protozoans, coccidian, or other harmful bacteria causing gastroenteritis/diarrhea. They tend not to eat, must be medicated, and may struggle to survive. These geckos could possibly cause health problems that might spread to other animals in your collection. Wild-caught Fat-tails should be completely isolated and quarantined, away from any other animals, until they are considered healthy.

Captive-hatched African Fat-tailed Geckos usually cost more, but are generally healthy and free from parasites or diseases. When selecting a Fat-tail, make sure the tail is plump and fat, it is alert with bright eyes, and has an overall healthy appearance. Inquire as to how the fat-tail has been housed and maintained. Most captive-hatched Fat-tails eat crickets, however, be sure to ask exactly what the gecko is eating and how often. If the Fat-tail is a tiny hatchling, inquire as to when it was hatched and if it has started to eat.

HOUSING and SUBSTRATE

African Fat-tailed Geckos can be housed in a similar environment to Leopard Geckos. Hatchlings and sub-adults should be housed in small enclosures. Small enclosures will give the young geckos a feeling of security and safety to avoid stress, and enable them to readily locate their food. An ideal enclosure for a single Fat-tail would be a 5-gallon (16" x 8" x 10") or 10-gallon glass aquarium (20" x 10" x 12") with a fitted screen top. The 10-gallon aquarium can sufficiently house three to five hatchlings or two to three sub-adults or one to two adults. Single hatchlings or sub-adults can also be kept in Rubbermaid® shoeboxes with a lid, providing sufficient air-holes are made for ventilation. Other enclosures similar in size are also adequate. The height of the enclosure is not critical for African Fat-tails as they are terrestrial geckos, or ground dwellers, and not arboreal, or climbers. Many gecko breeders use a rack system that utilizes either small Rubbermaid® shoeboxes or the 28 qt. plastic Rubbermaid® containers that enables them to house a large number of Fat-tails, singularly, or in groups, utilizing a minimal amount of space.

Typical setup for hatchling African Fat-tails. Photo by Lois Durflinger of L & J Reptiles.

The interior of enclosures for hatchlings or sub-adult Fat-tails, like young Leopard Geckos, should be simplistic. Paper towel for the bottom of the enclosure is recommended as the substrate. Add a small hide box and a shallow water dish. African Fat-tailed Geckos need more humidity than Leopard Gecko. To help keep the humidity at a higher level, place a small amount of Repti-bark®, orchid bark, or sphagnum moss in a small, flat container and place it at the cool end of the enclosure. Check the substrate often to make sure it remains damp all the time. The Fat-tail can decide if it wants to be warmer or cooler. Fat-tail enclosures can also be misted several times a week to keep the humidity level high enough.

Larger African Fat-tailed Geckos do very well housed in a 5- to 10-gallon glass aquarium. A 10-gallon aquarium will house two adult Fat-tails. A 20-gallon long or a 28 qt. Rubbermaid® would be a suitable enclosure size for three to five adult Fat-tails. Orchid bark, newspaper, indoor/outdoor carpeting, or paper towel can be used for the substrate. Orchid bark substrate can be kept damp by misting several times a week for sufficient humidity. If using newspaper, indoor/outdoor carpeting, or paper towels as the substrate, add a separate area with orchid bark or sphagnum moss. This can be kept damp at all times to provide higher humidity. Several hide boxes and a water dish, completes the setup. An additional hide-box, also serving as an egg-laying box, in the form of a plastic food container with a lid and filled with damp vermiculite should be added. Keep this container inside the enclosure all the time.

Note: When placing more than one adult Fat-tailed Gecko in an enclosure, make sure there is only one male. Males tend to become aggressive towards each other when they mature and can cause serious damage to each other.

African Fat-tailed Geckos need to be kept at a temperature of approximately 85° F at the warm end of the enclosure and 75° F at the cool end. A heat lamp or a regular 25-40 watt incandescent light bulb can be used for a heat source. Place the light over the top of the enclosure at one end. This will create a warm end and a cool end. The African Fat-tailed Geckos can choose where they are most comfortable. A heating pad, placed under the enclosure at the warm end, will supply added heat, but usually will not generate enough heat to achieve the ambient temperature of 85° F inside the enclosure. If using a heat lamp, closely monitor the heat so the enclosure does not overheat. An enclosure that is too hot or too cold will stress the gecko.

Most breeders that use a lidless rack type system use under-the-cage heat tapes and regulate the temperature with rheostats. If using this type of housing, check the temperature frequently to make sure the rheostats are working properly and the correct temperature is maintained. Being nocturnal, African Fat-tailed Geckos do not require a UV-emitting bulb. However, a red light bulb or heat light can be used to observe their nighttime activities. Never use a heat rock as they can cause severe burns to your Fat-tail. A lighting system on a timer set for 12 hours will provide a day / night cycle.

FEEDING

Captive-hatched African Fat-tailed Geckos generally have a staple diet consisting mostly of crickets dusted with a vitamin/mineral

A juvenile het for amelanistic striped African Fat-tailed Gecko. Photo by Ruben Lugo of Taino Reptiles.

supplement and calcium. Mealworms can also be offered, however, most Fat-tails seem to prefer crickets. It is important to gut-load crickets with quality nutrients before feeding them to your Fat-tails for added nutrition.

Hatchling Fat-tails should be fed daily with 1/8" to ¼" crickets. To determine the proper size of crickets to feed your Fat-tail, approximate the length from the eyes of the gecko to the snout. This will give you the size of cricket to feed as it will be smaller than the gecko's mouth and easy for it to eat and swallow. As the Fat-tails grow, larger crickets can then be introduced. I recommend feeding your Fat-tails in the early evening as they are awake, alert, and ready to search for their food. Remove any uneaten or dead crickets the following morning.

Make sure clean water is available at all times. Completely change the water at least twice a week and disinfect the water dish with a 1:10 bleach solution once a week. It is essential to maintain clean water to avoid growth of bacteria which can create an unhealthy habitat for the Fat-tail.

SEXING

Male and female African Fat-tailed Geckos are very similar in appearance to Leopard Geckos. Males have an upside down V-shaped row of 10 to 12 pre-anal pores just in front of the vent plus the presence of hemipenal bulges at the base of the tail. Females lack the pre-anal pores with no bulging at the base of the tail. Sexing African Fat-tailed Geckos can be done visually around the age of 3 – 4 months. Hatchling Fat-tails can be sexed by checking for the pre-anal pores with a 10x magnifying glass. However, this is very difficult and is usually only done by experienced breeders.

BREEDING

Breeding season for Fat-tails is usually in the late fall, starting around November and December. I recommend a cool down time with an ambient temperature drop to about 70° to 72° F (20.5° to 21° C) for about two months prior to the introduction of the male and female to each other. During the cool down time, no food is offered, but water should be available at all times. After the cool down period, the Fat-tails should go back on their regular feeding schedule. Egg-laying females should be given plenty of calcium to replenish calcium lost during egg production and food for energy.

Breeding groups of Fat-tails can consist of a pair, one male and one female, or, one male with four or five females, depending upon the size of the enclosure. African Fat-tailed Geckos do not breed as consistently as Leopard Geckos. Infertility tends to be a problem with many females producing no eggs or infertile eggs. Many breeders advise housing the females and males separately. During breeding time, place the male into the female's enclosure for several days then, remove him and place him back into his own enclosure. Repeat this process often during the breeding season. Make sure the egg-laying box, with damp vermiculite, is in the female's enclosure. Starting about two weeks after the Fat-tails have been placed together and have bred, start checking the egg-laying container several times a day for eggs. African Fat-tailed Gecko eggs tend to dry out fast, becoming non-viable eggs if not removed and placed in the egg incubation container.

"Pinkie" mice can be offered once a week to females which are laying eggs to give added nutrition and calcium for producing good calcified eggs.

Depending upon age, healthy and condition of the female, and fertility of the male, the female will lay a clutch of two eggs, about every 28 to 35 days. The female will lay her eggs typically two week to four weeks after copulation. The number of clutches varies and can be from only one clutch upwards to seven clutches.

EGG INCUBATION

African Fat-tail Gecko eggs are incubated the same way as Leopard Gecko eggs. Egg incubation containers, filled with damp vermiculite or perlite, should be prepared for the eggs. As with Leopard Geckos, the sex of Fat-tails is determined by incubation temperature. An incubation temperature of about 85° F (29° C) will produce both males and females. Lower temperatures, around 82° F (27° C), will produce mostly females, and higher temperatures, around 88-90° F (31-32° C) will produce mostly males. Incubation can be done on a shelf if the room temperature is between the required low of 82° F (27° C) and the high of 90° F (32° C). If using an incubator, set it up prior to the time to incubate the eggs to make sure the temperature is regulated before placing the eggs inside. A good but inexpensive incubator is the Hov-A-Bator®, which can be found at a farm supply center or on the Internet.

HATCHLINGS

African Fat-tailed Geckos hatch out at 45-60 days, depending upon the incubation temperature. Fat-tail hatchlings are smaller and more fragile than Leopard Geckos, and like Leopard Geckos, do not eat until 3-5 days after hatching. During this time, they live off the absorbed egg yolk. The Fat-tail will also shed first before starting to eat. It is recommended to keep the Fat-tail hatchlings on damp paper toweling in a shoebox enclosure that is kept warm. A small shallow water dish and a hide box should be included.

Crickets can be introduced after the hatchling has shed its skin. Cricket size should be approximately 1/8" to ¼" and they should be dusted with calcium and a vitamin/mineral supplement.

Hatchling African Fat-tails should be fed every day as they grow rapidly and need plenty of nutrition. Do not introduce too large or too many crickets as the fat-tail will become stressed and may not eat. Introduce about three crickets per Fat-tail if there is more than one in an enclosure. Any excess crickets should be removed by the following day. To determine the cricket size, estimate the length form the gecko's eyes to its nose. The cricket should be the correct size for the gecko to catch, to eat, and to digest.

DISEASES

Captive-hatched African Fat-tailed Geckos are hardy, acquiring few diseases. However, daily maintenance and care is required to insure that the Fat-tail stays healthy. Diseases and other health-related problems can be the same or similar to Leopard Geckos. Refer to the Health and Diseases chapter for signs of health problems.

A beautiful group of amelanistic African Fat-tails. Photo by Ruben Lugo of Taino Reptiles.

THE FUTURE

At this time, African Fat-tailed Geckos are still being imported, however, with the emergence of incredible new, beautiful color morphs, more herpetoculturists are beginning to take an interest in keeping and breeding them. In time, as with Leopard Geckos, importation will eventually cease and the African Fat-tail will no longer be taken from its wild habitat. It is impossible to speculate whether the African Fat-tailed Gecko will ever become a species found on the list of endangered or extinct species in the wild. Hopefully, its future is safe, at least for now.

No longer is the African Fat-tailed Gecko the "dark horse" of the gecko world. It has become a brilliant new star on the horizon and is providing challenges and excitement in world of geckos.

LEOPARD GECKO COLORS, PATTERNS, and MUTATIONS

Four genetic morphs currently being captive-bred: Normal (top), Blizzard (left), Albino (lower right), and Leucistic / Patternless (bottom). Photo by Robbie Hamper.

What a remarkable journey the Leopard Gecko has taken during its evolution from basic, non-descript imports, to today's Leopard Geckos that are spectacular crown jewels with indescribable brilliance! Even though wild-caught Leopard Geckos have been available in the pet trade since the 1970s, the so called captive-hatched color variations and "designers" first appeared in the early 1990s. Ron Tremper, through selective line breeding for many years, first produced normal Leopard Geckos with high yellow coloring. Then, a Leopard Gecko randomly hatched, exhibiting two longitudinal black stripes down the back with no normal banding. With further selective line and sibling breeding, Tremper produced the first reversed striped and jungle Leopard Geckos.

Credit goes to Tremper for demonstrating that pairing recessive genes, when line breeding or sibling breeding Leopard Geckos, results in selective traits for desired colors and patterns. In 1996, the first albino was hatched and in 1999, offered commercially for sale by Tremper. Tremper has been a tremendous influence and leader in Leopard Gecko herpetoculture, continuously producing exciting new genetic morphs and mutations.

During this same time, other Leopard Gecko breeders began producing new colors, and patterns, thanks in part to ongoing spontaneous genetic mutations. Leucistic, or Patternless, and the Blizzard, are two Leopard Gecko mutations currently available. At the 1995 Orlando Expo, Bill and Marcia Brant, Gourmet Rodent, introduced their brilliant tangerine/orange Leopard Geckos with tangerine/orange in their tails resulting in the "cheeto" color What an array of gorgeous Leopard Geckos never seen before! The surreal beauty of these Leopard Geckos awed reptile enthusiasts young and old! With the advent of tangerine Leopard Geckos, another new dimension and era opened up for Leopard Geckos to be produced with potentially infinite combinations of colors and patterns. Many breeders began to do specialized breeding for specific Leopard Gecko traits.

In the United Kingdom, Ray Hines began breeding for the tangerine color in the tails. Hines has successfully produced the "carrot-tail" line of Leopard Geckos. "Carrot-tail" geckos have intense tangerine/orange coloration extending down into the tail, varying from partial to complete coverage.

With the explosion of new color and pattern morphs, plus three mutations, Leopard Gecko terminology is increasingly becoming confusing. Listed below are some of the names, descriptions, and terms of Leopard Geckos currently on the market or future projects.

Mutation – A genetic change or alteration in a gene or chromosome creating a departure completely different from the parent but resulting in heritable characteristics.

Morph – Individual "natural" traits of the parents chosen by the breeder for selective line breeding to produce particular colors and/or patterns with the offspring resembling one or both parents.

MUTATIONS

Albino - A randomly genetically produced Leopard Gecko lacking melanin or black spotting resulting in red eyes with various banding colors. Currently there are three strains of albino Leopard Geckos lines, Tremper, Bell, and Las Vegas.

Leucistic/Patternless – A randomly genetically produced Leopard Gecko lacking melanin or black spotting with normal dark eyes. Hatchling are patterned but mature into white, gray, or yellow as adults. Originally referred to as Leucistic, but recently, referred to as Patternless.

Blizzard – A randomly genetically produced Leopard Gecko (from Mark and Kim Bell of Reptile Industries) lacking melanin or black spotting with dark blue/black eyes. Some consider the Blizzard a true leucistic. Two variations of the Blizzard are: Banana Blizzard – Blizzard bred with Patternless/Leucistic – yellow coloration, and the Blazing Blizzard – Blizzard bred with a red-eyed Albino (Bell Line).

COLORS

Amelanistic - Lack of melanin or pigments that account for dark color. In Leopard Geckos and Fat-tail Geckos, the lack of dark spots or patterns.

Axanthic – Minimal amount or lack of yellow, orange or red coloration. Color is white/grayish background with dark spotting. Selective breeding Axanthic parents will result in Snow.

Carrot-tail – Orange/tangerine color extending from the base of tail of the Leopard Gecko down into the tail area.

Designer - Any Leopard Gecko that is a different color from the normal.

Ghost – Pale to faded coloration, lacking dark pigmentation.

High Yellow - Intense bright yellow coloration, with or without spotting.

Hybino – Selective breeding of Albinos with Super Hypo Tangerine, Ray Hines line.

Hyper – Excessive amount of coloration.

Hypo – Minimal amount of dark spotting. Spotting: approximately 6-10 scattered spots with mostly solid color.

Hypo Gold Albino – Gold colored albino leopard gecko with no spotting, Ray Hines line.

Hypo-Tangerine – Tangerine colored Leopard Gecko with minimal dark spotting

Hypo-Yellow – Various shades of yellow, from light to dark, with minimal amount of spotting.

Lavender – Shades of lavender/purple appear on the body and tail of the Leopard Gecko with body colors of various shades of yellow or cream. Hatchlings display normal banding with the lavender color appearing as they mature.

Mack Co-dominant Line - Black and white Leopard Gecko with minimal amount of yellow, solid black eyes.

Mack Super Co-dominant Line – A true Axanthic Leopard Gecko – black and white, showing no yellow, solid black eyes.

Mack Pastel Snow Line - A normal pastel Leopard Gecko crossed with a Mack Co-dominant, producing a pale snow gecko with lavender blotches.

Mack Paradox – Leopard Gecko with longitudinal color discrepancies down entire body. Black on one side and light yellow on the opposite side, black spotting on both sides and two different colored eyes.

Melanistic – Dark coloring, almost completely black, or black with some gray, displays little pattern

Normal – Various shades of pale to bright yellow, light to dark gray.

Orange – Leopard Geckos displaying more orange coloration than yellow but not tangerine.

Red Racing Stripe – Tangerine Leopard Geckos with two deep red/orange dorsal lines down the back

Snow – Leopard Geckos with normal dark spotting, but on a white background. Jungle or Striped morphs can be Snows.

Sunglow - Selective breeding of Albino hypomelanistic carrot-tail Leopard Gecko. The Urban Gecko line.

Super-Hypo – No spots on body and head or no spots on body but some spotting on the head.

Super-Hypo Tangerine – Solid tangerine colored Leopard Gecko with no dark spotting.

Super-Hypo Tangerine Carrot-tail – Solid tangerine colored Leopard Gecko with tangerine/orange color extending down into the tail.

Super-Hypo Tangerine Carrot tail (Baldy) – Tangerine Leopard Gecko with a carrot tail absolutely no spots on the body or head.

Super-Hypo Albino Tangerine Carrot-tail – Solid tangerine colored albino Leopard Gecko with tangerine/orange in the tail and no dark spotting.

Super Hypo Albino Tangerine Carrot tail – Tangerine albino Leopard Gecko, with a carrot tail.

Tangerine – Intense, brilliant deep orange/reddish orange coloration, with various degrees of dark spotting to no spotting.

Yellow – Leopard Geckos normal coloration, ranging from light yellow to bright yellow but not the intense High Yellow.

PATTERNS

Baldy – A Leopard Gecko lacking spots or blotches on the head.

Circle Back – Circle pattern on the mid-back area of Leopard Geckos, outlined in black.

Designer – Any Leopard Gecko that is a different pattern from the normal.

Dorsal Striped Tangerine – A distinct white strip down the middle of the back of tangerine Leopard Geckos, starting from the neck to the base of the tail.

Hyper – Excessive amount of dark spotting.

Hypo – Minimal amount of dark spotting or coloration – Spotting: approximately 6-10 scattered spots with mostly solid color.

Jungle – Irregular patterns consisting of broken black dorsal bands, appearing as asymmetrical blotches and designs. Has a non-ringed tail. Colors range from gray, cream, light yellow, high yellow, tangerine, or albino.

Patternless – A phase now applied to the "Leucistic" Leopard Geckos. However, patternless geckos lack melanin, exhibiting no black spotting or pattern but colors ranging from brown, dark olive green, cream, white, gray, or yellow. Has normal eye color. Other patternless Leopard Geckos occur but are from different genes than the "leucistic".

Reduced Spotting – Less dark spotting than normal but more than Hypo or Super-Hypo.

Reverse Stripe – A dark longitudinal stripe down the middle of the Leopard Gecko's back stopping at the base of the tail. Tail displays no banding but blotches outlined by black. Hypo-Tangerine or other morphs and mutations can show stripes in various shades of dark orange, reddish brown, or white.

Striped – Leopard Geckos exhibiting a middle longitudinal stripe running from the white neck band to the end of the tail. The middle color ranges from gray, light yellow, to brilliant high yellow. The tail can appear blotched, partially striped, or completely striped.

Super-Hypo (Baldy) – Absolutely no spotting on head or body.

Two-Three Lined Striped - Several dark longitudinal stripes down the back extending to the base of the tail. Tail displays no banding but blotches or pale. Hypo-Tangerine or other morphs and mutations can show stripes in various shades such as dark orange, reddish brown, or white.

PHOTO GALLERY

A group of high-yellow Leopard Geckos showing some of the variety in pattern. Photo by Robbie Hamper.

Two circle-back Leopard Geckos. Photo by Robbie Hamper.

Jungle Leopard Gecko showing the irregular dorsal pattern and unusual coloration. Photo by Robbie Hamper. Animal courtesy of Raymond Ditmars Bruckman.

Jungle Leopard Gecko showing the irregular dorsal pattern and Glow Yellow coloration. Photo by Robbie Hamper. Animal courtesy of Raymond Ditmars Bruckman.

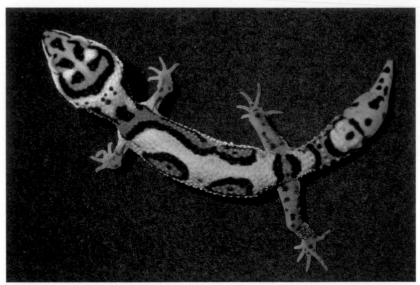

Jungle Leopard Gecko showing the irregular dorsal pattern and High Yellow coloration. Photo by Robbie Hamper. Animal courtesy of Reptiles By Mack.

Jungle Red Racing Stripe Leopard Gecko showing the irregular dorsal pattern and no banding on the tail. Photo by Robbie Hamper. Animal courtesy of Jeff Galewood.

A striking juvenile lavender Leopard Gecko. Photo by Robbie Hamper. Animal courtesy Raymond Ditmars Bruckman.

A beautifully patterned Mack Co-dominant Leopard Gecko. Photo by Robbie Hamper. Animal courtesy of Reptiles by Mack.

An intricately patterned Bell Albino Leopard Gecko. Photo by Robbie Hamper.

One of the hottest new morphs of Leopard Gecko is the Blazing Blizzard. Photo by Bill Love. Courtesy of Mark and Kim Bell of Reptile Industries.

Genetic Giant Leopard Geckos. This new mutation was bred and developed by Ron and Marilyn Tremper. Pictured are "Moose" (right), at three years of age, next to his one-year old son. Both weighing 150 grams and still growing. Photo by Ron Tremper.

A ghostly Albino Leucistic Leopard Gecko. Photo by Robbie Hamper. Animal courtesy of Reptiles by Mack..

A high yellow albino Leopard Gecko. Photo by Robbie Hamper.

An orange albino Leopard Gecko. Photo by Robbie Hamper.

A beautiful powdery orange Tangerine Leopard Gecko. Photo by Robbie Hamper.

A young Carrot-tail Super Hypo Leopard Gecko. Photo by Ron Tremper.

A beautiful Super Tangerine Albino Leopard Gecko. Photo by Alberto Cadolini of A & M Gecko .

A stunning Tangerine Albino Jungle Leopard Gecko. Photo by Alberto Cadolini of A & M Gecko.

One of the most unusual color / pattern morphs available to future hobbyists is the Mack Paradox Leopard Gecko. Photo by Robbie Hamper. Animal courtesy of Reptiles by Mack.

An open striped lavender Leopard Gecko. Photo by Robbie Hamper. Animal courtesy of Raymond Ditmars Bruckman.

A Tangerine striped Leopard Gecko. Photo by Albey Scholl of Albey's "Too Cool" Reptiles.

An exciting new morph for the future - the Red Racing Stripe Leopard Gecko. Photo by Jeff Galewood, Jr. of JMG Reptiles.

Super Hypo Carrot-tail Leopard Gecko. Photo by Albey Scholl of Albey's "Too Cool" Reptiles.

A Gold Hybino Leopard Gecko. Photo by Ray Hines.

An adult Mack Co-dominant Pastel Snow Leopard Gecko. Photo by Robbie Hamper. Animal courtesy of Reptiles by Mack.

A spectacular Hypo Snow Leopard Gecko. Photo by Craig Stewart of The Urban Gecko.

A striking Snow Leopard Gecko. Photo by Albey Scholl of Albey's "Too Cool" Reptiles.

A Mack Super Co-dominant Leopard Gecko is a ghostly snow phase gecko with an unusual linear spotting pattern. Photo by Robbie Hamper. Animal courtesy of Reptiles by Mack.

In nature, Fat-tailed Geckos are found in either a banded or striped form. These traits are being manipulated by those involved in breeding these geckos. Photo by Robbie Hamper.

An adult female amelanistic Fat-tailed Gecko. Photo by Ruben Lugo of Taino Reptiles.

A stunning adult male amelanistic Fat-tailed Gecko. Photo by Albey Scholl of Albey's "Too Cool" Reptiles.

A beautiful orange and lavender amelanistic Fat-tailed Gecko. Photo by Robbie Hamper. Animal courtesy of A & M Gecko.

BIBLIOGRAPHY

Allen, R. 1987. Captive care and breeding of the leopard gecko *Eublepharis macularius*. In: Reptiles: Proceedings of the 1986 UK Herpetological Society's Symposium on Captive Breeding.

Balsai, M. 1993. Leopard geckos. Reptiles and Amphibian magazine. Mar/Apr 1993: 2-13.

Bartlett, R. D. and P. Bartlett. 1999. *Terrarium and Cage Construction and Care*. Barron's Educational Series, Inc. Hauppauge, NY.

Black, J. 1997. Keeping and Breeding Leopard Geckos (*Eublepharis macularius*). Reptiles March 1997: 10-18.

Both, A. *Geckos, Rare & Common*. Reptiles Quarterly. T.F.H. Publications, Inc. Neptune, NJ.

Brant, W. E. 1994. Leopard Geckos. Reptiles April 1994: 4-8.

Brant, W. E. 1995. Leopard and Fat-tailed Geckos. Reptiles USA Annual 1996: 4-8.

de Vosjoli, P. 1990. The General Care and Maintenance of Leopard Geckos and Fat-tailed Geckos. Advanced Vivarium Systems, Lakeside, CA.

de Vosjoli, P., R. Klingenberg, R. Tremper, B. Viets. 1998. The Leopard Gecko Manual. Advanced Vivarium Systems, Inc., Santee, CA.

Funk, R. S. 2002. *Lizard Reproductive Medicine and Surgery*. Vet. Clin. Exot. Anim. 5, 579-613.

Gamble, T. 1997. A Leopard Gecko (*Eublepharis macularius*) Bibliography. privately published. Bloomington, MN.

Puente, L. 2000. The Leopard Gecko. Howell Book House, Hungry Minds, Inc. New York, NY.

Tremper, R. 1996. Leopard Geckos: Past and present. Reptiles USA Annual 1997: 136-143.

Tremper, R. 1997. Designer Leopard Geckos. Reptiles March 1997: 16.

Viets, B. E., A. Toussignant, M. A. Ewert, C. E. Nelson, and D. Crews. 1993. Temperature-dependent sex determination in the leopard gecko, *Eublepharis macularius*. Journal of Experimental Zoology 265(6): 679-683.

ECO WEAR & Publishing

We bring you Books , T-shirts and Hats that celebrate
the reptiles and other wildlife you love!

www.reptileshirts.com   517-487-5595

915 Seymour, Lansing, MI 48906